Turbocha...

Networking

How to Go From Jobless to Building Relationships with Super Achievers

By

Tallal Gondal

TO SUMMER

MAY YOUR HEART ALWAYS

SHINE IN THE DARKEST OF

TIMES.

i

Praise

"My students and I have learned really valuable lessons on networking and generous human connections from Tallal. He certainly walks the talk: not only did he share his expertise in a superbly articulate manner, but he also showed us through his interactions with us how the best kind of networking is to be implemented. I would definitely recommend Tallal Gondal's "TurboCharged Networking" to anyone who needs to upgrade their human connection skills. I think that includes most of us."

Francisco Vergara
Professor
FRVM
National Technological University
(Argentina)

"Tallal is supportive and thoughtful to your first steps in networking needs. The information he shares is applicable in a variety of networking settings and easy to follow. Having put filters in place as Tallal suggested, I have done the impossible, created more time in my day! I look forward to reading his new book 'TurboCharged Networking' and how I can apply similar strategies in expanding my motivational speaking opportunities."

Robin Matrai
Motivational Speaker
www.robinmatrai.com

"When Tallal moves, join him or get out of the way!"
Yvonne Dyson
Holistic Therapist
http://thebeyond.co.nz/

"Tallal initially started as a client of mine. Our business relationship became a sort of Mentor-Mentee relationship as I was looking to expand my business. His clear instructions and advice were fantastic. His constant enthusiasm and passion to help shape someone to be the best were inspiring to say the least. It's no wonder he wrote a book that could become a Bestseller. Clear and concise details on how to build and maintain relationships and get forward in business, it's a fantastic read. I definitely recommend TurboCharged Networking."
Adnan Khan
Islamic Finance Coach
adnankhanfsblackburn@gmail.com

"I have had the pleasure of having consultations with Tallal and have found each one very rewarding. I usually have a list of ideas on which direction to take my business, but Tallal collates the ideas and forms a simple clear set of objectives to work towards to ensure those targets have direction and are met. After consulting with Tallal, I have the clouds removed and a few new gears I didn't know I had. After reading an extract from the book, it reads like having Tallal there giving you the new ideas, the motivation and direction to take things further."
Dale Mason
Founder at Beardo Weirdo

"I first met Tallal during a digital event a few months ago. There was such a 'resonation' to the information that he presented on TurboCharged Networking. What really struck me was the reality that I had been spreading my effort for building my spiritual business 'so thin' as I had been trying to network with so many groups and others that really were not aligned with what I was trying to develop.

His simple statement of looking at one's circle of influence and who are the 5 main people you spend the most time with and the fact that you are the average of them, well - what did that mean for me - yikes - I have been spending time with those that don't even know my spiritual and transformational journey. No wonder I felt deflated at times after spending time with them, family or not.

After my one-on-one call with Tallal, which was truly eye-opening, I am super excited to read his book and implement his recommendations - I have no doubt my networking techniques will be upgraded! A sincere 'Thank you Tallal' for sharing such amazing insights on TurboCharged Networking."
Lois Warnock
Spiritual Psychic Artist and Medium and
Energy Healer
loiswarnock@telus.net

"I'd describe my first meeting with Tallal as being given an injection of 100% positive energy. I'd challenge anyone to spend an hour in his company and not feel inspired. I was particularly drawn to his high energy and enthusiasm. I'd absolutely recommend Tallal as a motivational coach and can't wait to get my hands on his soon-to-be-published book Turbocharged Networking."
Tony Mendez
Senior Sales Executive

"Tallal's mindset is so clear, he can elucidate complex relationships and break them down into simple easy to understand chunks. His knowledge in the world of networking is superb and his desire to always be improving is to be admired. He helped me understand the benefits of different relationships and has put me on a path to improve the ones I have and the ones I want to have in the future."
Jamie Patel
Treasurer at Leicester Leaders Speakers

"It was a pleasure to talk with Tallal and he really puts his words to action when he says comes from a place of service. Tallal shared his networking experience and how to build a solid reputation when starting in a new team, which has helped me tremendously. I can't wait to read Turbocharged Networking when it comes out."
Riten Solanki

"The talk that we had with Tallal Gondal, it was very interesting and useful for me because he caught my attention when he told us about the importance of how to communicate with other people and the way in which it can help us to progress in any situation.

Personally, I recommend his sessions because, although for me it was the first time to hear and know him, it left me very interested in reading his book 'TurboCharged Networking' and learning about his way of thinking."

Nancy M (Trainee Teacher at ENS Totoral College, Argentina)

Cover design at Canva.com

ISBN: 9798737402785
Imprint: Independently published

Before You Read...

To download the *Swipe File* with all the examples/templates and the *Recommended Reading List* use this link:

https://bit.ly/2VEF1sW

About the book

I have written this book in my 'voice' and as a conversation between the author (me) and the reader (you). This is because I want you to 'hear' my voice in your mind whilst you read and experience what it would be like if we were having a conversation sitting together and enjoying coffee.

Also, I wrote this book based on my experience and what I learned and discovered on my journey. I completely understand that there are other methods, strategies, and points of view. If discover something that complements or enhances anything that I have shared with you, then use that alongside what is in this book. At the end of the day what really matters is that you get results that TurboCharge your life and your business.

Speaking and Coaching

For inquiries about having me speak at your event and coaching opportunities, please send your email to: TurboChargedNetworking@gmail.com

Don't forget to leave a stunning 5-star review on Amazon and share this book with anyone who will benefit from this message.

Table of Contents

Foreword by Corey Poirier

When I first discovered this thing called Networking, I couldn't have done it more wrong if I tried.

I thought somehow it was all about seeing what I could get from the other person, and never even tried to make it about them, or even really learning anything about them personally, or their needs.

I struggled of course because I was trying to make it all about me - it never occurred to me that it may not be the way to build real relationships.

I was in sales at the time, and I was simply in it to see if I could find new clients.

I didn't.

Fast forward a few years and I found myself networking again – this time I was doing it as part of a non-profit leadership group I was the President of and I really wasn't doing it to build the business.

Surprise, surprise – this time, when I was making it about the other person and how I could serve and support them, business flowed. The more I tried to give, the more people wanted to support me and my business.

This is how I learned what networking really is, and should be.

Well, this and reading Bob Burg's powerful book about the power of being a Giver, The Go-Giver.

This is also why, when I first met Tallal Gondal, the first thing that struck me was his willingness to ask what he could help me with, and his commitment to standing behind that offer.

It's sadly rare to see someone offering to give before asking.

As I've noted, I didn't even do it myself in the beginning, and yet, it is one of the key traits of the networkers who are welcomed, and have an audience, in basically any circle.

This is to say, Tallal truly gets what networking is all about.

First, he offered to feature me on his show.

Then he offered to connect me with others in his network.

The offers kept coming and at no time did he ask for anything in return.

Again, this is a rarity in the influencer space.

The end result is that I wanted to see him succeed at the highest level and in return offered to connect him with others and feature him on our platforms – simply because he was doing what few will; and it stands out.

This one trait alone, not including everything else he knows and has learned about networking in the years since, makes him THE person to write this book.

It's also the exact reason I was excited to contribute the foreword to this book – because Tallal truly practices what he preaches.

This book, which you now hold in your hands, holds the secrets and clues, as the subtitle says, *to Go From Jobless to Building Relationships with Super Achievers.*

You might call this book, liquid gold – and not only because it contains the wisdom to help you build a better life and business, but also the keys to achieving the fulfillment a person can only truly experience when they are a giver.

And with that, I'm going to leave you in very capable hands.

I hope this book transforms your life forever, and I hope it brings you as much abundance (and not just in financial wealth) as networking has brought me.

Yours in success,
Corey Poirier
bLU Talks Founder and # 1 Barnes and Noble, Amazon, and Kobo bestselling author

Introduction

Congratulations on purchasing this book and consciously taking the steps to learn one of the most important skills in this life: Networking and building relationships.

You are here because, like me, you believe in the Jim Rohn quote, *"You are the average of the 5 people you spend the most time with."*

BOOM!

Mike drop...

And, like me, you also believe that the only difference between you and the Super Achievers of this world is; what they know and what they do with what they know.

The simple fact is that if you had access to the Super Achievers then you could follow in their footsteps and achieve the exact same results that they have managed to achieve.

Let's quickly define what I mean by a 'Super Achiever'. I define a Super Achiever as someone who has found a MASSIVE amount of success and has created EXTRAORDINARY results in their life, business, industry, or field. They could be a celebrity, a sports person, an entrepreneur, a leader, an influencer, a top executive, a CEO, or a Nobel Prize-winning academic. Some examples of famous Super Achievers are:

- Elon Musk
- Richard Branson

- Dwayne 'The Rock' Johnson
- Tiger Woods
- Beyonce
- Oprah Winfrey
- Warren Buffett

However, they don't need to be world-famous to be a Super Achiever. My definition doesn't include a popularity rating, instead, it focuses on the results that they have managed to create for themselves.

I believe that our goal should be to achieve holistic success, however, we all cannot be experts in all areas of life. It is impossible for us to be experts in parenting, relationships, finances, business, investing, psychology, child development, creating strong habits, creativity, productivity, health and fitness, nutrition, spirituality and faith, social media, marketing, education, etc. However, by connecting and building relationships with top experts, leaders, and influencers in different areas we can learn from them, follow their footsteps and TurboCharge all areas of our lives and our businesses.

The main problem that we all face is that we don't really know where to _find_ these Super Achievers, how to make contact and _connect_ with them, and finally, how to _build relationships_ with them so that we can become a part of their '_Inner Circle_' and they can become a part of ours. If you are wondering the same things, then you are not alone. But it's not your fault. We were never taught these skills at school.

Recently, my friend Rachel Randolph, who is a Communication Coach for self-starters, organised a LinkedIn survey to find out what is people's biggest struggle with building professional/personal relationships. The results were pretty shocking! 29% of the people who participated voted 'Social Anxiety' as their biggest problem, 34% voted for 'Maintaining the connection', 10% voted for 'Don't know how to meet people' and 26% voted for 'Burnout from work/life'.

There are countless people and companies offering to help everyone grow their network and meet their ideal client/person. However, that was the least-voted struggle. Only 10% of the people said that they are unsure of how to meet people. 90% of the people don't have that struggle. 63% of the people struggled with 'Social Anxiety' or were not sure how to 'Maintain the connection' and build relationships. However, there is hardly any focus on these two critical issues that are affecting nearly two-thirds of the people!

Can you relate?

Are you also shocked by these statistics?

This is precisely why I decided to write this book. To give the average person the skills to create, with time, energy, patience, focus, determination, effort, and hard work, their own advantage in life, career, and business. Throughout the book, I will share with you lots of examples of how to approach different situations and what to say to address any issues around 'Social Anxiety'. I will also share advice on following-up and I have dedicated an entire chapter to 'Staying in Touch' to equip you with the tools to 'Maintain the connection'.

Regardless of whether you are a student feeling lost about your next steps, an aspiring entrepreneur who is unsure about where to begin, feeling stuck in a corporate job, a business owner who has hit a plateau, a self-improvement junkie feeling stagnant, or a stay-at-home mom looking to find a new identity, this book will help you develop the confidence, mindset, and skills to find, connect and build relationships with anyone, anywhere, at any time.

I have not written this book as a checklist with a pile of *'dos'* and *'don'ts'* for networking success and neither is it an essay where a ton of information is dumped upon you that leaves you completely overwhelmed and unable to have clarity and make decisions and move forwards. Instead, it is a step-by-step program that will help you to cultivate the mindset and also develop the skill set needed to become a world-class networker. A mindset that will help you achieve success in all areas of your life. A skill set that can be used over and over again, adapted to suit your unique situation, and molded to meet your particular needs.

This book will show you where you will find the Super Achievers and 'Unreachables' of the world. It will also give you strategies to leverage your social media for networking. You will learn how to network effectively in person, during meetings and events. There are also advanced strategies to TurboCharge your networking journey and access to a recommended reading list and message templates that I have personally used. Visit the link on "Before You Read" - page viii to download the *Swipe File*.

I am super excited for us to take this journey together and I am really looking forward to reading your success story one day. During this journey I want you to keep an open mind and genuinely be curious about everything that I will share with you in this book because using them has allowed me to build a solid world-class network for myself. As a result, I was able to access amazing opportunities, which included collaboration and investment opportunities, behind-the-scenes conversations with experts, exclusive coaching calls, and advice from top achievers. I was featured, multiple times, on The Mentee podcast (one of the top Business podcasts on iTunes) and was the finalist for hosting Season 3 of The Mentee.[1]

I was also featured in *The Book of Public Speaking* by Corey Poirier (international bestselling author and multiple times Tedx speaker) and also on Corey's radio podcast *Get Paid to Speak*. I had the honour of speaking at the bLU Talks *Amplify Your Message* event in December 2020, alongside top influencers, leaders, and experts in their respective fields. It also allowed me to bring on world-class guests on my YouTube show, which I started as a hobby, and interview them.

However, I started from absolute Zero, not knowing anything about networking and building relationships. In June 2015, I was made redundant without any warning. I had a young family and my daughter was born just a few months before. I was scared. I was overwhelmed with stress. I felt completely helpless. I needed to provide for my family but couldn't see a way forward. I was just a Maths Tutor. I had no other experience outside of my job. Yet, I knew that networking was important for creating and gaining access to new opportunities because that's what I had witnessed by watching other people accelerate. I realised that I needed to surround myself with powerful people so I can create opportunities for myself. At the time, I was surrounded by people who were at a similar stage

---

[1] https://thementee.com/

in life and had similar circumstances. They didn't have the answers to my questions or the solutions to my problems.

I felt pressure when I saw others who had a network because not only did I not have a network, I also didn't know how to start building one. I felt lost and doubted myself and believed that I don't have a network because I am not good enough. I also felt like a failure because I believed that I should be able to figure out the secrets to networking and being highly connected, yet nothing changed. The worst bit was that I felt stuck because I didn't have any answers and I definitely didn't have a plan.

Maybe you feel the same. Maybe you are standing at the sidelines, watching others accelerate. Maybe you haven't tried anything yet because you are also feeling lost. Or maybe you did try in the past, but things didn't work out the first time. Maybe you are feeling stuck where you are in life and are wondering, "What if...?"

The most important difference from where I was, to where I am now, is that now I am surrounded by lots of super successful people and I can turn to them whenever I need help, support, and advice. For example, this is my first book. I am a first-time author and I have never written a book before, let alone have any idea of how to pitch, market, and promote it. And there have been plenty of times when I got stuck, made mistakes, and needed help, advice, and support.

Before I probably would have tried my best with what I know to overcome these obstacles, maybe do some research, gotten stuck, and eventually given up on writing this book. Now, I reached out to people in my network who were International

Bestselling Authors and enlisted their advice and support. They helped me reframe my thinking, shared their insights, expanded my mind, and challenged me to grow far beyond my comfort zone. The clarity, focus, and value that I got from those conversations were absolutely pivotal in making this book possible. This is the power of networking, building relationships, and surrounding yourself with powerful people and I am going to share with you what I have learned through my journey.

However, I can share everything I know about networking with you, all the strategies, tactics, insights, and tips, however, you need to take responsibility for your own decisions and results in life. I can teach you everything I know, but unless you consistently take action, you will not get the results. You need to make the commitment to act on everything that you learn.

"Consistency is what transforms Average into Excellence." *Anonymous quote.*

So, don't delay in reading this book and taking action on the strategies that are shared with you. The sooner you begin the better and the sooner you would begin to create your own extraordinary results. Remember, you are trying to learn a skill set, which takes time and effort so the earlier we start, the bigger the impact we can make.

"The difference between Dreams and Reality is called Action." *Anonymous quote.*

The best advice I can give you right now is:

• Don't focus on the end result. Focus on Mastering the skill. Most people have the misconception that they need to *achieve* their goals. We don't achieve our goals. We grow into them.

● Take the emotion out of the process. Right now, you are excited because you just bought this book and you are motivated to start and dive right in. However, over the days, weeks, and months that excitement will die out, so unless you cultivate discipline and develop the right habits, you will not achieve success.

● There will surely be times, whilst reading this book, when you think to yourself, "That's obvious!" or "That's so basic!" or "I knew that!" or "I could have figured that out!" If these are all true then why haven't you still achieved the results? I will tell you why, because common sense is not common practice. It takes a lot more than just knowing something to act on it effectively and create extraordinary results. Trust me, I experienced this first hand as I was writing this book. There were so many times when I overlooked simple basic ideas and advice and got stuck or made mistakes. It's true that you can't read the label if you are in the box.

● Set specific goals and actual deadlines for each goal. If you want to achieve success then you need to have clear goals and take action consistently. For example, your goal might be to read a chapter of this book each day, but you also need to put a deadline on it. "By _____ I will act on what I have learnt from this chapter."

● Don't give up just because something didn't work the first time. You are learning something new, and as with learning anything new, failure is a part of the journey. Just because it didn't work the first time, it doesn't mean that it will never work or that the strategy is flawed. Flip the strategy and attack again. That's how winning is done!

• Once, you have decided on your goals and established routines and habits, maintain them and do not let small challenges stop you. THERE ARE NO EXCUSES!

• Celebrate your victories. If you do manage to connect with a Super Achiever and secure them as your mentor or you form a partnership etc., make sure to share all your wins. Even the small ones. Remember, you are the hero/shero of your life.

As I said before, I would love to read your success stories and connect with you. I am always keen to know how my students applied this knowledge and created extraordinary results for themselves. So, reach out and share.

Finally, I want to congratulate you again on purchasing this book and on making the decision to invest in yourself.

"Heroes are ordinary people who make themselves extraordinary." Gerard Way

PART I: Cultivating the Mindset of a World-Class Networker

In order to TurboCharge your life, you need to find, connect and build relationships with the Super Achievers of this world and learn directly from them. You can then follow in their footsteps and achieve the same results that they have managed to achieve. In Part 1 I am going to share the fundamental basics of networking with you. Everything else that we are going to learn will be based on these foundations.

Here we are going to start by gaining clarity on what kind of Super Achievers we need to invite into our lives. Clarity is not something we are born with. Like wisdom, clarity is achieved through careful thought and purposeful experimentation. The best way for us to gain clarity is to ask high-quality focused questions and dig deep.

"Knowledge is having the right answer. Intelligence is asking the right question." Bhavika Jain

Chapter One: The Foundations

"You are the average of the 5 people you spend the most time with." Jim Rohn

I first heard this quote in 2016 whilst listening to season 1 of The Mentee podcast, hosted by Geoff Woods, at home. It blew me away. I stopped everything. I grabbed a piece of paper and a pen and I made a list of the 5 people in my life that I was spending the most time with.

Now it's your turn. Use the spaces below to make the list of the 5 people you spend the most time with.

1. _____

2. _____

3. _____

4. _____

5. _____

Great! Now I want you to ask the following 2 questions that I asked myself after I made my list.

➢ Are the people on your list where you want to be in life/career/business/impact/relationships/influence/spirituality …?

If not, then this is where this book comes in. I will show you how exactly you can upgrade your 5, because if your 5 have not already achieved the results that you want to achieve then how can they help, guide, support, and mentor you to your success???

The second question that I want you to ask yourself is:

> Do they build you up or tear you down?

Seriously, be honest, do the people on your list push you forward, drive you, motivate you, and elevate you or do they tear you down. As important as it is to upgrade the five people you spend the most time with and build relations with the Super Achievers, what is equally as important is to let go of the *rotten apples* that hold you back and tear you down.

Sometimes, it's really hard to let go because they are our friends or our family and we can't just let go of them entirely. And I don't want you to cut off all your relations, but I do want you to be honest with yourself and realise that they are holding you back. You may not be able to control the people in your life, but the one thing that you do have control over and the one thing that you can act on immediately is to limit your exposure to them. Limit the time that you spend with them and create as much distance as you can healthily manage.

I asked myself these exact questions after making my list and I acted on the advice that I am sharing with you myself. Sometimes these decisions are hard, but they are absolutely necessary for TurboCharging your life.

"One of the hardest decisions made in life is to choose which bridge to burn and which bridge to cross." Anonymous quote

The *Art* and *Science* of Networking

The number 1 thing that you need to realize about networking is that it's both a *Science* and an *Art*.

15

It's a *Science* because there are some 'Golden Rules' that you must follow if you want to be successful at networking. These 'Golden Rules' are universal for everyone, regardless of who you are, where you are from, and must always be followed.

However, networking is also an *Art* because your style of networking will be truly unique to you, depending on your personality, goals, passions, and also where the Super Achievers of your chosen area of focus hang out.

All this comes together to form your unique style of networking that you will develop over time and, like the tide, will change depending on where you are in your life and the goals that you are pursuing. It's something that you definitely discover and develop over time and it will take effort and patience because what you try might not work the first time or it may not work at that time or it might not work because of the strategy that you used. But if you don't give up and keep trying different ideas and strategies, eventually you will discover the right one that works and yields extraordinary results.

By going through this process, you will discover lots of new and exciting things about yourself and your networking style. Don't let small failures stop you. Failures only tell you what doesn't work, they don't signal the end of the world. We will get to the 'Golden Rules' a little bit later.

"There is no such thing as failure, only feedback." Brian Tracy

Circles of Life

Let's look at the different areas of your life and identify which of these areas need attention. Doing this will allow us to work out what kind of Super Achiever you need to invite into your life. This exercise will give you the sniper-shot view of the areas of your life that require the most focus. For example, you might want to start a business and so you need to find, connect and build relationships with top entrepreneurs and business owners. On the other hand, your friend might be struggling with his/her marriage and instead needs to invite top marriage and relationship coaches/therapists into his/her life.

Not doing this will result in a shotgun approach where, potentially, we invite everyone into our lives regardless of whether their presence will actually make a difference or not. This is not smart and neither is it a strategy. It is, however, chaos.

If we are going to put time, effort, energy, and money into something, we need to make sure that it yields the results that we actually desire.

Let's have look at the different areas of your life that might need TurboCharging:

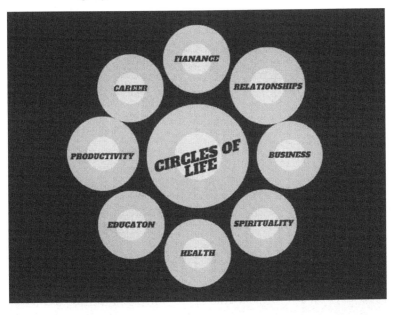

This list is not exhaustive. You can add any other areas that are not on the list.

We, as humans, will move towards something that causes pleasure and will move away from something that causes pain. Aristotle, in his 'Rhetoric', suggested that pain and pleasure occur on a continuum. He described it very much like a push-pull concept. Therefore, in order for us to identify the target areas of your life which will benefit the most by connecting with a Super Achiever I want you to think of the following:

➤ In which area(s) am I facing challenges, problems, or resistance?

➤ In which area(s) do I have goals, aspirations, and dreams?

Now, for any *challenge* area(s) of your life, you need to understand this Universal Law of Tallal: *Every problem is a people problem.* (The fireworks go off; everyone stands up clapping furiously and I am awarded the Nobel Prize)

Virtually any problem that you have in your life, can be solved if you had access to the right people in your life. They will either solve the problem for you themselves or tell you how to solve the problem yourself or direct you to a place or resources where you could go to get the problem solved. You just need access to the right person who is an expert in that field. That's what's missing from your life right now. So, let's make a list of the top 3 problems that can be solved immediately if you had access to the right person.

1. _____

_____

_____

2. _____

_____

_____

3. _____

_____

_____

Time to look at your goals, which brings us to another Universal Law of Tallal: *Every goal is a people goal.* (The cameras roll, flashes fill the scene, I kneel down and the Queen of England awards me Knighthood)

Virtually any BHAGs (Big Hairy Audacious Goals) that you have, can be achieved by having the right people in your life. Again, they will either help you achieve your goal themselves, or tell you how to achieve your goals yourself, or direct you to a place or resources where you could go to achieve your goals. So, just like before, let's make a list of the top 3 goals that can be achieved immediately if you had access to the right person.

1. _____

_____

_____

2. _____

_____

_____

3. _____

_____

_____

Finished? Excellent! All of this is critical information that will inform you of what kind of Super Achievers you need to connect and build relationships with. I want to stress this because I believe that this is an important point to understand. The reason that we struggle with our problems and our goals is that we obviously do not have the knowledge and skills to work on them and neither do the current people in our network. This is because our network is mainly made up of people who share our 'Sphere of Influence'.

Let me quickly explain what I mean by 'Sphere of Influence'. It includes people within 3 levels of separation from us: Level 1 - our family and friends. Level 2 - family and friends of people in Level 1. Level 3 – family and friends of people in Level 2. These people are probably at a similar stage in their life, have similar circumstances and similar experiences to us. Therefore, it is very unlikely that they will have the answers that we seek. As a result, to get the answers that we are looking for, we need to expand our network and our Sphere of Influence to include the people who come from a different 'world' than ours and, ideally, have already achieved success in the areas that we need help with. We are more likely to find the solutions and the answers to our questions outside our Sphere of Influence.

In *"High Performance Habits"*, Brendon Burchard highly encourages adding new people to our existing network in order to boost our social environment and gear it towards our success. He refers to a phenomenon called 'Clustering', where our social environment and the people in our Sphere of Influence directly affect our health, behaviours, life circumstances, level of achievement, and happiness, both positively and negatively.

The effects of 'Clustering' cannot directly be observed or measured, without taking a detailed inventory of the behaviours, health, and levels of achievement and happiness of everyone in our Sphere of Influence. Therefore, 'Clustering' occurs beyond our conscious observation and so, it is absolutely critical that we are very careful and strategic about who we are spending our time with and who is allowed to enter our social environment.

The final thing that we need to do before finishing this chapter is to create a *Profile(s)* of the Super Achievers we are trying to connect with. A *Profile* is a detailed description of the kind of person you need to invite into your life who can help you solve your problems and/or achieve your goals.

This is the stage where we need to get hyper-clear on who exactly do we want to build a relationship with. If we are not clear on this then all our time, energy and efforts will go to waste because we will just be shooting at a moving target in the dark with a blindfold on whilst spinning. We want to be intentional about growing our network and expanding our Sphere of Influence so that it serves us, not just in the short run, but also in the long run.

"There is nothing as intense as a moment of clarity when you suddenly see what's truly possible for you." Anonymous quote.

When writing the *Profile(s),* we also need to consider the Relevance of Scale. This refers to the fact that the advice of someone who is a few steps ahead of us is going to be a lot more relevant and beneficial, compared to the advice of someone who is lightyears ahead.

Typically, we all want to connect with and learn from the top most successful people. However, that is not always the best course of action because someone who is at the top is operating at a completely different scale that is beyond our current comprehension. We need to seek advice and guidance from someone who is operating at a slightly higher scale than us and can turn around and help us navigate the same path successfully.

Let's say that I start a YouTube channel and I want to get lots of subscribers. I have a choice to either connect and get advice from a successful YouTuber with 5 million subscribers or a successful YouTuber with only 5,000 subscribers. Initially, it might seem like a great idea to connect with the YouTuber with 5 million subscribers, however, their advice will probably be more relevant after I have already got 500,000 subscribers or more.

On the other hand, the advice of someone with 5000 subscribers is going to be a lot more relevant and immediately useful to me. Moreover, the Super Achiever with 5000 subscribers will probably be easier to get a hold of and probably will be more willing to help, compared to the Super Achiever with 5 million subscribers.

Ok, let's go back to the lists of your top 3 problems and goals, and based on these, write down, with as much detail as possible, the description of the person who might be able to help you find solutions and create extraordinary results. Create a profile for each problem and goal individually. It is ok if they overlap as the same person might be able to help you with multiple problems/goals. Think about the following questions as you write your descriptions.

➢ What unique knowledge do they need to have?

➢ What unique skills do they need to have?

➢ What experience do they need to possess?

➢ How would they be able to help you?

➢ When do you need their help, advice, and support?

Do things seem to be coming together? Can you see the fog lifting? Does it feel amazing to have such a high level of clarity? At this point, you totally have my permission to throw your muffin at the far wall and shout "Heck Yea Baby!" Just do so without saying anything if there are other people around you, or actually throwing any muffins. I don't want them to think that we are weirdos, just in case they are a secret Super Achiever who we need to connect with later. Best not risk it...

TurboCharged Takeaways

➤ Look at the list of the 5 people you spend the most time with and evaluate their impact on your life objectively. Do you need to upgrade your 5? How are you going to deal with the *rotten apples?*

➤ Networking is an Art and a Science and it will take some time and effort to discover and develop your unique networking style

➤ You are going to develop a new skill set and doing so will involve failure, effort and patience. Acknowledge this and get comfortable with this truth.

➤ Use the Circles of Life to identify exactly which areas of your life do you need help with the most.

➤ Identify your top 3 challenges and your top 3 goals in life and get hyper clear on what kind of Super Achievers you need to connect with.

➤ Create a detailed profile for each type of Super Achiever you need to connect with and identify the platform where you can go to find them.

In the next chapter, you will learn the Golden Rules of networking without which you will not find the success you are looking for. You will also learn the #1 Magic Question that you can ask, which will allow you to connect with any Super Achiever.

Chapter Two: The 'Golden Rules' + The Magic Question

"You have to learn the rules of the game. And then you have to play better than anyone else." Albert Einstein

As I sat down to make a list of these rules to share with you, I had to replay every interaction I had ever had with a Super Achiever, both successful and unsuccessful, so I could extract the core lessons and the overall governing forces of those interactions and summarise them for you into a list of simple rules. (Wow, this is a long sentence. But who cares as long as it makes sense, right?)

So now a headache and several frown lines later, I am happy to announce that the list of these 'Golden Rules' is ready for your consumption. They must be followed by one-and-all at all times regardless of who you are, where you are from and what you have managed to achieve in life so far. Following them will take your networking skills to new heights that you never previously thought were possible.

The 'Golden Rules'

> **Divorce your ego**

First impressions are everything, which is why it's critical that we set the right intention before connecting and interacting with others. It doesn't matter what you have managed to achieve and what results you have managed to create; you have to show up in the world as the best version of yourself. Don't think of networking as a tit-for-tat or give-and-take transaction. A lot of the time we enter a conversation or interaction with an agenda and a sense of entitlement. This is extremely toxic for networking and building relationships. No one wants to connect and be around someone who is only there to get something for themselves. You have to be authentic and show up as someone who truly wants to be there to connect with others. You must be present. Don't be tempted by short-term temporary gains. Lose your ego and any sense of entitlement when connecting with others and you will build a strong community around that will help you thrive in your life and your business.

> ## Be more interested than trying to be interesting

Instead of doing a recital of your life's story or a list of your achievements, be genuinely curious and find out about the other person. What are they working on right now? What are their interests? What are they passionate about? What are their struggles? What are their challenges? Where do they need help? The key here is to get the other person to talk and share what is important to them. Everyone likes to talk about themselves. As a matter of fact, people have over 6000 thoughts per day and most of them are about themselves. We as humans are deeply concerned about ourselves. To build rapport and connect deeply, you need to consciously direct the focus on the other person.

> ## Come from a place of value and service

Always think about how you can help the person you are trying to connect with. The quickest way to build a relationship with anyone is to help them with something that they are struggling with or to help them gain clarity on something that they are uncertain about. Everyone has struggles and challenges regardless of who they are and what they have managed to achieve. We are all human at the end of the day. You must help them first, before having any thoughts about them helping you. During every interaction, always ask yourself:

"How can I add value to this person right now?" "How can I serve them best?"

Imagine that you are wounded, hurt, desperate and bleeding. Suddenly, everything and everyone shifts out of your focus. All your attention is on your wound and on finding a solution to stop the bleeding. There might be people around your trying to distract you or trying to provide moral support, but to you it's all irrelevant, unless one of them actually has a solution to your predicament. At that moment, the only person you would want to speak with is someone who can help you.
Always keep this in the back of your mind when you are interacting with others.

Here is a testimonial from Vaibhav to illustrate this. Our supposed-to-be-15-minute call turned into over an hour-long coaching session after he mentioned that he has an idea for a business, but he doesn't know how to get started. I immediately offered to help by sharing how he can get started.

"I was supposed to have a 15-minute chat with Tallal which ended up being over 1 hour long. In that time, Tallal massively over-delivered. So, he definitely practices what he preaches! During our call, Tallal helped me to develop a strategy on how I can start building a list of potential clients for my coaching business, but also told me what I should say to start building a relationship. Tallal's biggest strength was his ability to understand my discomfort in calling strangers and was able to guide me into the right mindset by sharing his own experiences of building relationships with high-net-worth individuals."

Vaibhav Vadera
Fearless Living Coach
President of Leicester Leaders Speakers
LinkedIn: @viabhav-vadera

➢ Be Genuine and Authentic

Not only do people hate someone who is being fake, but they can also tell when someone is being fake. How can they conjure such magnificent magic? Intuition. Oh yea! Every one of us has built-in instincts that help us accurately make judgements about the intentions of others. This is precisely why First Impressions are so important.

According to a 2016 study on intuition from the University of New South Wales, we can use unconscious information in our body or brain to help guide us through life, to enable better decisions, faster decisions, and be more confident in the decisions we make. The study also found that intuition improves over time, suggesting that the mechanisms of intuition can be improved with practice. So, there you have it, be genuine and don't fake it. People can tell the B.S from the truth. Be present, with an open mind, an open heart, and be in a place of giving, so they can see that you are truly interested in them and you truly want to invest in the relationship.

"Every interaction requires a new great First Impression."
Tallal Gondal

➢ Be curious

I know I have said it before, but this is definitely worth repeating. Be genuinely curious and find out more about them. What is their main focus right now? What's exciting about what they are doing? Why do they do what they do? Just come from a place of curiosity like a child, and find out as much as you can about the other person, without being too intrusive or creepy. Don't be pushy or come across as a bully. Don't ask personal or private questions. Just stick to good open-ended questions that get the other person to talk and share. You want to create a deep meaningful conversation and you want to leave them with a great experience to remember.

➤ Be Patient

If you are someone like me then you absolutely dread the word 'patience'. I am not a man naturally blessed with an abundance of patience and hearing this word is an instant source of anxiety. As I was going through the process of learning, testing and improving my networking skills, I consciously had to discipline myself and continue marching forward, despite encountering a ton of failure along the way, especially at the start. Prepare yourself for a similar fate as it takes time, effort and lots of patience to learn a new skill set and then use it to create extraordinary results.

Gene McNaughton is one of the leading business growth experts and has spent more than 25 years generating top results for Fortune 500 companies, including helping grow Gateway Computers from a small company that was founded on a farm, to an $11 billion international powerhouse. Gene was also the Executive Vice President of Sales for Tony Robbins' companies, and he shattered sales records with Tony for the 3 years he was there. I finally managed to get an interview with Gene for my YouTube channel in November 2018 after chasing it for almost 2 entire years! That's 730 days of failure, hustle and patience that no one knows about.

➤ Smile 😊

If I have to explain this one to you, I am literally going to get up and beat you with an onion. That way it won't be clear why you are crying.

When you smile, the other person can't help but smile back. It's natural. It also gives the subconscious impression that you are warm, friendly, confident and are willing to be the first to 'break-the-ice'. It also proves that talking to you will not result in those 'awkward moments'. Smiling helps the other person to drop their guard as they feel that talking to you would be safe, comfortable and adventurous. They see you just as another person, like them. Remember, regardless of what we have achieved, we are all still human.

If you are not communicating in person or via video, then try to capture your smile in the message, email or the tone of your voice in an audio call. The smile must be present in the tone of the message. You want to make the other person smile as they respond to you. It might help to smile whilst you type your message or take an audio call.

The 'Magic' Question

This, this is pure gold. It's the one question that you can use to put everything we have covered so far into action, effortlessly. This question will differentiate you from 99% of the herd, the millions, who are also after that elusive Super Achiever. They are also trying to connect and build relationships with the industry leaders, top CEOs and influencers. But they don't have this book so they are probably going to just try to talk about their own life's story and then try to jam their business card or their contact details in the hand of that Super Achiever. And they might even succeed in achieving this, but trust me, they will never get anywhere. They should really read this book.

"WHAT ARE YOU WORKING ON RIGHT NOW AND WHERE DO YOU NEED HELP?"

Yup, that's it. That's the magic question. Take a moment to just marvel at the genius behind this question. (Holding your breath in awe and angels singing in the background are optional)

This question embodies everything that we have covered so far. Divorcing your ego, being more interested than trying to be interesting yourself, coming from a place of giving, being genuine and authentic, showing that you are truly committed to building and investing in this relationship and being curious.

Ask this question to everyone that you meet and watch as the magic happens right there in front of your eyes. The 'Magic' question helps you to find out their pain points, what is their top priority right now and what challenges are they facing. Then, you can start thinking about helping them. We will discuss this in more detail later and I will show you how you can actually help them. But this question is the gateway to forming a relationship with any Super Achiever. This is the exact question that I ask every time I meet someone new and it has helped me to build a world-class network and surround myself with some of the most successful people in the world.

Remember, on top of all the commitments and responsibilities that a Super Achiever might have in their life, everyone is fighting for their attention. Everyone else just wants to get something for themselves; a job, an opportunity, money, recognition, a promotion, a contract... But you are the one person who comes to them with an offer to help, with curiosity, without being selfish and without any ego. You immediately stand out.

"A person's biggest asset is not a head full of knowledge, but a heart full of love, an ear willing to listen and a hand willing to help others." Sushil Jain

In the last chapter, we identified your top 3 challenges and goals and we want to make sure that you are able to TurboCharge those areas of your life with the help of the Super Achievers you are connecting with. But before all that, comes the relationship that you form with them, which, if you play it right, will last you a lifetime. You want to still be friends long after your challenges are over and your goals are achieved and to do so, you need to invest in the relationship by helping the other person and prove your commitment. Now you are someone who is valuable to them. Someone they actually want to be friends with and stay in touch with.

Let's dig deeper. I will share with you a technique that I have developed that will transform you into a Networking Ninja. When you first connect with a Super Achiever, they might not open up to you straight away because you are a stranger to them. At times you might find that they themselves are not clear on their challenges and areas of focus. So, to overcome this, the strategy that I have developed is this: reword the question and ask it at different times. This will allow you to stay focused on the main priority of getting to know the other person, whilst giving you time to build rapport and trust.

Here are my versions of the 'Magic' question. You are welcome to come up with your own.

➤ What is your main focus right now and where do you need support?

➤ What is your biggest challenge at the moment?

➤ What main projects are you focusing on right now?

➤ In what area do you need the most support?

➤ What is the one thing that will make the most difference to your business/job/project right now?

➤ What type of support will allow you to meet your deadline/key targets/major goal?

> What are your plans for the future?

> Where do you see this business/career/project going in 'x' weeks/months/years?

A while ago, I put up a post in one of the online communities that I was a member of. Lots of people replied and were excited to connect and were inspired by what I was working on at the time. One of the people, Kai Whiting (profile on - page 160), replied to my post and said that he wanted to connect me with a Super Achiever, Don Wettrick (profile on - page 159), which he very kindly did, without asking for anything in return. I sent an email back thanking him and asking him about his current focus and where I could help him in return. He did not reply back. I proceeded to connect with Don and we became friends quickly and I interviewed him for my YouTube show.

Again, I sent a "Thank You" email to Kai and asked about his work and where he needed help. This time Kai replied and said that he wants to do a Skype call. (Ha, Skype! Remember those days?) During the call, Kai told me that he has been working on a project and he has been waiting for a sign to partner with someone on this project. However, he didn't find anyone and no one offered to help and despite him not replying to me initially I was still here asking him about his work and offering to help. Kai saw this as a sign and offered me the opportunity to work with him on that project there and then. In the end, we did not work on that project together, however, that opportunity would never have come by if I hadn't come from a place of service.

I got multiple wins from one social media post simply by following the 'Golden Rules' and coming from a place of authenticity, curiosity and giving. I made two new friends, I got a great interview for my YouTube channel and also an opportunity to work on a project which never would have happened otherwise. Kai's decision to offer me the opportunity was not a random one and the opportunity coming my way was not a 'lucky break'. It was all a product of purposeful consciously directed focus and effort. When Kai didn't reply the first time, I didn't give up. Instead, I followed up.

Similarly, Kai connected me with a Super Achiever without any expectations. He just wanted to help because when he read my social media post, his intuition (we looked at the evidence on this from the scientific study earlier) informed him of my authenticity. He trusted me not to mistreat the person that he was connecting me with, despite the fact that he had never met me before.

"You can make more friends in two months by becoming interested in other people than you can in two years by trying to get other people interested in you." Dale Carnegie

The Possible Solutions

At this stage, you might be wondering, *"What can I possibly help these Super Achievers with? They already have an amazing team working for them. They already have a world-class network of their own. They probably know about more ideas, people and resources than I am even aware of. What would I do if they actually do ask me for help with something that I don't know about?"*

Valid thoughts, I grant you that. However, you are forgetting that before this, they didn't have **you** in their life. And before this, you hadn't read this **awesome** book. Let me explain…

These thoughts of inadequacy and feelings of limitation are:

34

a. Quite normal

b. Only there because you think that you have nothing of value to offer. Your mind is trying to preempt a possible threat and so your threat alarm system is going cuckoo.

The fact is that you actually have no evidence to support these thoughts or feelings. How could you possibly know that you are not going to be able to offer any value to someone without actually talking to them and finding out what they need? You are just doing a status comparison in your head and logically concluding that their status is beyond your current status and so you are ill-equipped to help them. It is only your perception of the situation, rather than the real situation itself that's making you think this way.

Here are some of my strategies that will allow you to think beyond your limiting thoughts and feelings and instead will positively direct your mind to focus on finding opportunities and solutions. Just remember to ask yourself these questions whenever you are in a conversation with someone (They don't necessarily have to be a Super Achiever every time. They could even be your mom. I would have used a *scared emoji* here, but I ran out at Halloween).

➢ Can I help them myself?
Here, think about any ways that you can directly help the other person yourself.

➢ Can I connect them with someone I know already who might be able to help them?
You might not be able to help them directly, but you might know someone who might be able to. Think deep here.

35

➢ Can I direct them to a place or a resource that will solve their problem(s)?

Rack your brains for any services, service providers, products, or online resources, blogs, articles, websites, books, podcasts that might be useful.

➢ Can I learn the knowledge and the skills to solve their challenges?

It certainly requires more time, effort, energy and commitment than the others, but definitely something that you might consider.

You will be surprised because as you start to connect with different people, you will be able to connect one person with another because you can see that they're a perfect match. You know they can work together on collaborative projects, business, hobbies, skills or experiences, etc. and you will certainly become a person of value to both. Also, you will hear about the different systems and resources that different Super Achievers are using and so you will be able to pass on this knowledge when you come across someone who needs them.

Homework

For your homework (Ha, you thought I would forget!), I want you to ask the 'Magic' question to everyone you meet for a whole week and try to put these principles into practice. Ask this question to at least one person every day for an entire week and then follow through; try to help them with their projects and challenges. It will make it more natural for you to ask this question without having to divide your mind and exert effort when you are standing in front of that Super Achiever. With practice, you can just be present and curious during your conversation instead of trying to figure out when and how to ask the question and then try to think of your responses to their answer.

Don't miss this step! You want to come across as a 'Pro' who can navigate the turbulent waters of professional and business networking with effortless ease. You will start to see the elegance with which ideas and opportunities start to fall at your footsteps.

"Practice does not make Perfect. Practice makes Permanent."
Eric Thomas

Remember, only you, and you alone, are responsible for the results in your life. It's time to take action and attack this because without action there are no results.

Action Deadline

When setting the deadline for this homework, I want you to write a clear detailed daily plan that you will follow. You can complete the following sentence, *"I am committed to..."* by inserting the exact actions that you will complete each day in order to keep progressing towards achieving the final goal of completing this homework e.g., *"...I will set a reminder on my phone to appear 3 times during the day to ensure that I am not forgetting to ask the 'Magic' question to the people I meet. At the end of each day, I will take some brief notes to evaluate the day and make sure that I follow through with any promises that I made to help people. Therefore, by (insert future date) I will have completed all my homework."*

Just setting a deadline without a clear step-by-step plan will just set you up for failure even before you start. This is the main reason most people fail in taking consistent action and meeting deadlines. They never formulate and write the exact plan with granular details.

"I am committed to…

_____

_____

_____

_____

_____

Therefore, by _____ I will have completed all my homework.

TurboCharged Takeaways

➤ Follow the 'Golden Rules'. Remember to always:

o Divorce your ego
o Be more interested than trying to be interesting
o Come from a place of value and giving
o Be Authentic and Genuine
o Be Curious
o Be patient
o Smile 😊

➤ Ask the 'Magic' question to everyone you meet. Rephrase and ask at different times to build rapport.

➤ When connecting with someone new remember to ask yourself:

o Can I help them myself?
o Can I connect them with someone I know already who might be able to help them?
o Can I direct them to a place or a resource that will solve their problem(s)?
o Can I acquire the knowledge and the skills to solve their challenges?

In the next chapter, you will learn how to leverage different mediums and platforms to identify the Super Achievers in your area of interest and the specific strategies to find and connect with them.

Chapter Three: Finding the Super Achievers

"Life is all about finding people who are your kind of crazy."
Anonymous quote.

"Where do I go to find these amazing Super Achievers?" I hear you ask. *"I'm not even sure who the Super Achievers in my area/field/industry are. If only I knew who they are and where they hang out, I would swoop in like a Master Networking Ninja and use everything I have learnt from this awesome book to charm the socks off them (*Yes, socks! We are trying to be decent here.*) I would make you proud, Tallal. So proud!"*

Don't worry. I hear you. So here are some tips:

➢   Books.

"But I don't like reading books!" Just suck it up and get over it already. Stop being a baby and start acting like a mature responsible adult. What is wrong with people? Do you ever turn to your doctor and say, *"But I don't like taking medicine because it smells funny?"* Well, guess what, you are reading a book right now!

Anyways, reading top-selling books in your area/field/industry is a very good place to start. The authors themselves and any people who are interviewed, mentioned, or featured in the books are very likely to be the Super Achievers you are looking for.

> Podcasts

There are literally hundreds of thousands of podcasts out there, virtually on every conceivable topic/area/field. There are podcasts on everything from children's psychology and economics to entrepreneurship and homeschooling. So, it's very likely that there is a podcast out there on the area you are interested in or the field that you want to explore. The podcast hosts themselves and the guests that they bring on are all likely to be Super Achievers.

> YouTube channels

There are a ton of YouTube channels churning our billions of hours of footage every day. Go to YouTube and search for the key terms related to your topic/area/field/industry and make a list of all the people who are featured or interviewed on these channels. You can also reach out to the YouTube hosts themselves.

> TV/News

There exist a boatload of dedicated TV channels and TV shows for specific interests/fields that could be your primary research ground for Super Achievers. Are you interested in sports, cooking, starting a business, or relationships? What's new in the news regarding your chosen area of interest? There will be something on the TV to point you in the right direction.

> Newspapers/Magazines

Newspapers have sections and columns on a wide variety of topics. There are even newspapers and magazines about specific areas e.g., health and fitness, property, fishing, trains…. you get the idea.

➢ Blogs

They are everywhere. And they are about everything, which makes them an awesome resource to exploit in your search for Super Achievers. (Now there are even microblogs!) Find a reputable blog and reach out to the blogger and any guests who are featured/mentioned.

➢ Websites

Just Google the keywords related to your chosen area/topics and a house-load of websites with all the profiles, interviews and articles will pop up. Are all of them going to be mega amazing for finding Super Achievers? No! Is it worth checking out the few good ones? Yes!

➢ Ask others

The easiest place to start is to ask the people around you (family, friends, colleagues, neighbours, etc.). We usually massively underestimate the value of our current network, but if you ask, you would be surprised how quickly you will find out about different Super Achievers. Ask the names of leaders and experts who you should look out for and follow. If someone has any connections, ask if they will be willing to make an introduction. You might have to return the favour in some way, but it would be worth it.

These are not the only ways to research, identify and find the Super Achievers. You can use whatever other means and platforms that you are familiar with, are willing to try and actually yield success. The main thing is that you get results. How you achieve them is not that important in this case.

What next?

Once you have identified the Super Achievers, you need to find them on social media platforms such as Facebook, Instagram, LinkedIn, Pinterest, Twitter, etc. Certain Super Achievers prefer certain social media platforms, so search for them, find them and follow them. I will give you the strategies for specific social media platforms later. For now, it's important that you identify and follow them on social media so you can get exposure to their world and their lives. Familiarise yourself with their interests, routines, ideas, hobbies and the people in their inner circle. Get to know the complete person, not just see them as a 'means to an end', how everyone else sees them. Obviously, don't be weird and act like a stalker. Observe and interact conscientiously. You want to gather information about them that will give you a solid ground to start that initial conversation and build a relationship.

You can also attend any events and conferences that they might be attending or are likely to attend. If you can't find anything about events on their news feed, then you can simply Google the keywords to find local/national events that they might be speaking or delivering at. Events and conferences are another great resource, as all the Super Achievers are going to be packed together in one physical space at the same time. I will give you the strategies to network during physical events later in the book. Just hang tight for now...

Another great idea is to join online communities and groups. Again, we will cover this in more detail later. You might not be able to attend an event or conference where you can share the same physical space, but you can still share cyberspace with them. You will be part of the same community and you will be able to see what kind of posts they are putting up and what they are working on right now.

You can also join local and national networking groups. Very likely, there will be a group(s) that meets up from time to time near you. Again, Google is your friend. (Google should really sponsor this book after this many plugs!)

Some of these online communities and local/national networking groups might be paid ones. (No, you don't get paid. You have to pay them.) Either way, you can explore your options and decide what works for you.

Managing Expectations

Ok, we have covered a lot, but I feel that it's my responsibility to share a few words of wisdom with you.

Firstly, do not expect immediate results. Don't expect them to respond to you straight away. Some might not respond at all initially (like Kai didn't) or at all, ever. I have certainly had to deal with this many times, where I never got a response despite following up and sending 4 or 5 messages. Obviously, I didn't send all 5 messages in one day. I spaced each of the messages by 2/3 weeks. I realised that they have very busy schedules and so I gave them plenty of time to respond each time.

Ideally, you should never give up. Instead, try taking a different approach such as finding them on a different platform, connecting with the people around them instead of directly connecting with the Super Achiever, or attend the same physical/virtual event that they are attending and connect with them there. There is always something else you can try. We will discuss all these strategies in more detail later in the book.

If you do manage to get some responses, then that's great. But, despite the responses, don't expect them to start a relationship straight away. If you sense some distance or hesitation, don't worry about it. Just be polite and respectful and go with whatever level of interaction they are comfortable with. You need to allow some time to build rapport and trust. The fact that they responded to you is a big achievement in itself. They get pitched all the time, from every direction, every day. Be patient. Don't overwhelm them. Be curious and show your interest in them. Try to find ways to help them because that's how you can show that you are willing to invest in the relationship and that's how they will see value in you.

(Honestly, if only half the relationship gurus, therapists and dating websites shared only half of this advice, the world would be a better place.)

Ok, so let's assume that you did get some responses, you have built rapport and trust and you are fast making friends. This is fantastic news, but don't expect to have all your problems solved and all your goals achieved immediately. It will happen organically, over time. Right now, your priority is to build that rapport, trust, and a relationship with them. You want to engage them so that they continuously want to have a conversation with you.

I know we did that exercise earlier, where we identified your main challenges and goals, but that exercise was there just to help you to get clarity on which Super Achievers do you need to connect with to TurboCharge your life. You don't get to throw your list in front of your new contact straight away and demand their advice, time and expertise. The idea is to build a relationship and help them so that they are willing to reciprocate. That's when you get to share some of your list with them.

Making the 'Ask'

Obviously, you can't wait forever for them to ask you how they can help you. What if they never ask? The main thing to remember is that there is a right time to make your 'Ask'. Personally, I believe that it's best to delay making the 'Ask' for as long as you can and in the meantime, focus on adding value and invest in building the relationship. However, there are times when you do have to be daring and make the 'Ask' because sometimes it takes courage to take a risk and just 'Ask' to get the results. However, your focus should always be on adding value first.

Once again, don't expect immediate results. Actually, it's best to give them a way out and give them the chance to say 'No' when making your 'Ask'. You can say something like, *"There is no expectation here. I completely understand if you say 'No'. It will not affect our friendship and I will still continue to find ways to help and support you."*

It makes them feel safe, in case they are not comfortable dealing with your request at that time or if they just don't want to do it. They might say that they are busy right now and or find some other way of letting you know that they can't deal with your 'Ask' right now. Just be polite, thank them, say that you understand their situation and that you would be grateful if they can consider your request when they are able to. You can always follow up and send them a polite reminder when the time comes. In my experience, most people will respond to your request and help you because they are keen to add value back to you.

Michael Roderick (founder of Small Pond Enterprises, founder of ConnectorCon and host of *Access to Anyone* podcast) refers to this as the 'Reciprocity Impulse', where people whom you help, actually want to help you back and are keen to return the 'giving gesture'.

During my interview with Michael[2], he told the story of how he came up with the idea of ConnectorCon and then reached out to his network with the proposal of them being part of the conference and because of their strong 'Reciprocity Impulse' and willingness to give back, Michael was able to plan the whole conference in 2 hours! He was then able to sell and execute the very first ConnectorCon within 35 days. Of course, Michael had added value and built relationships with all these people before making the 'Ask' and they were happy and keen to help Michael when he approached them with his proposal.

It's easy to fall into the trap of always giving to others without ever asking for anything yourself. There certainly is a lot of advice out there about 'giving' and whilst I believe that it's important to give, it is also important that you 'Ask' so you can overcome your obstacles and achieve your goals.

Michael suggests that you establish all your relationships from the start in such a way that it's clear to other people what you are trying to achieve in life. He believes that it's important to strike a healthy balance between 'giving' and 'asking'. Otherwise, if you are only giving to others, you can end up burning yourself out. The term that Michael uses is 'The Giver's Fix'. According to Michael, we get a release of 'feel-good' chemicals whenever we give to others, however, we do not get this release when we ask. Therefore, a lot of people just end up constantly giving to others because they keep experiencing that 'rush', but they don't take care of themselves and as a result don't do that well in business and in life and just burn themselves out.

Here's something to keep in mind when you do finally make the 'Ask'; you definitely do not want to come across as 'entitled' or 'desperate'. The best way to frame your 'Ask' is to

---

[2] https://youtu.be/9Qbeh_Uei7E

pose it as a problem/issue that you are facing and ask for their views on what would be the best way to solve it. You want them to willingly offer the 'solution' to you and framing the 'Ask' this way offers them the opportunity to 'rescue' you without making them feel uncomfortable and making the situation awkward. Michael definitely endorses this and so do I.

So, to recapitulate, have the courage to make the 'Ask' when the time is right, frame it as a problem that you are seeking their opinion on and offer them the opportunity to come to your 'rescue' willingly.

My main aim in networking is to build as much 'Relationship Capital' as possible by investing in the relationships and keep my 'Asks' to a minimum. This is because my main focus is always to establish a strong long-term relationship. As a result, I have gained a reputation for being very generous, giving and being a 'SuperConnector'. Although, I do have to admit that I don't make the 'Ask' as much as I should and I recognise that I do have to work on this.

Build Instant Rapport and 'Likability'

A TurboCharged tip that I can share here is that whenever you connect with anyone for the first time, try to look for common areas of interest to instantly build rapport and be likeable, instead of focusing on the differences. The saying, "Birds of a feather, flock together" is very true. We as humas prefer to be around and be friends with people who are 'like us' and have similar interests. Let me share a personal example. I love cats. I am a total cat lover, so if during a conversation someone tells me that they have a cat or they also love cats, I totally melt in puddles of joy fuelled by cat love and we usually spend ages talking about our cats, sharing stories and our favourite memories of our cats.

48

On the other hand, if someone tells me that they love dogs, I just replay with, "Cool. Personally, I am a cat person. Tell me about your dog(s). What are they like?" or "Sweet! What makes you love dogs so much?"

In summary, when you have common areas of interest, the conversation will flow smoothly. When there are no common areas of interest, just be curious and ask why they are interested in whatever it is that they are into. There is no need to highlight the differences and suffer through awkward silences or Sudden Conversation Death.

If you have any great stories about Sudden Conversation Death, you can share them with me at *TurboChargedNetworking@gmail.com*. I would love to read them and maybe we can even share a few laughs in private.

Homework

Your homework here is designed to help you get started and gain momentum in talking to people and putting these strategies into action so that you feel more comfortable and confident. Confidence comes from competence and to gain competence at anything you will have to do deliberate practice with repetition.

"Repetition is the mother of mastery." *Tony Robbins*

Make a list of 5 people that you feel comfortable talking to below. Just 5 people that you wouldn't mind calling on the phone to have a conversation with. Family, friends, or anyone you know really well will work absolutely fine. (BTW you can totally do more than 5 people if you want to)

1. _____

2. _____

3. _____

4. _____

5. _____

Great! Now I want you to go down your list and at least call one person every day. However, instead of repeating the dialogue to a normal conversation, you are going to consciously and purposefully direct the conversation to a more productive path. Here is what a normal conversation looks like:

You: Hey, how are you doing?
Friend: I'm good thanks. How are you doing?
You: Yea, I'm good too. What's new with you?

Friend: Oh, not much, just the same old... What's new with you?

You: Oh, not much. Just tagging along... What are you up to?

Friend: Oh, not much right now. How about you? What are you up to?

You: Oh, not much...blah blah blah...

You are not going to lose any ounces of brain cells in this type of (insert appropriate insult here) conversation. Heck no! Here's how you can direct the conversation to a more productive path:

You: Hey, how are you doing?

Friend: I'm good thanks. How are you doing?

You: Yea, I'm good too. What's new with you?

Friend: Oh, not much, just the same old... What's new with you?

You: Quite a lot actually. I am working on a new project that I am super excited about. Right now, I am looking to surround myself with people who (insert the details of the type of people you are trying to connect with e.g., "are investing in real estate"/ "have their own online business" / "homeschool their kids" etc.)

Now just be silent and wait. No, you do not need to fill the silence. Let that sink in. Allow them time to process and respond.

At this stage your friend will either:

➢   Know someone who meets the profile of the person you are trying to connect with and if so, you can ask if they are willing to make an introduction. You can also ask how they would like the favour to be returned.

51

➢ Don't know anyone who meets your profile, but they are curious and want to know more about your new project. Be excited and tell them what they want to know. Don't worry, your comments will stick in their mind and when they do meet someone who fits the profile, they will remember you. Preempt by asking them to arrange an introduction when this does happen.

Starting small and having these conversations with your family and friends will develop your thinking and allow you to be creative in a familiar and comfortable environment. Eventually, when you do reach out to the industry leaders, top influencers and other Super Achievers you will be operating as a Networking Alchemist with clarity, focus and confidence. You might find it useful to take some brief notes and evaluate how each conversation went and how you can improve it next time.

Action Deadline

Again, write a clear detailed daily plan that you will follow by completing the following sentence, *"I am committed to…"*, here insert the exact actions that you will complete each day in order to keep progressing towards achieving the final goal of completing this homework e.g., *"…messaging 3 friends, during breakfast, to see if they are free to talk for 10 mins after 6 pm today, tomorrow and the next day and add these reminders to my phone calendar. During the call I will use the script above and afterwards I will write some brief notes in my planner to evaluate the calls and see how I can improve next time. Therefore, by (insert future date) I will have completed all my homework."*

"I am committed to...

_____

_____

_____

_____

_____

_____

_____

Therefore, by _____ I will have

completed all my homework.

TurboCharged Takeaways

➤   To identify the Super Achievers in your area/interest/field/industry

- Read top-selling books
- Listen to the top podcasts
- Scour the big YouTube channels
- Watch relevant TV programs and news reports
- Read newspapers/sections/columns
- Read the best blogs
- Hunt on the related websites
- Ask people around you

➤   To connect with the Super Achievers:
- Find and follow them on social media
- Attend conferences and events
- Join online communities and groups
- Join local and national networking groups

➤   Don't expect immediate results

➤   Don't expect to have your issues addressed immediately

➤   Be patient

➤   Continue to be curious, add value and invest in building the relationship

PART II: Leveraging Social Media

In Part 1 we covered the basic essentials for cultivating the mindset of a world-class networker. Here, in Part 2, I am going to share with you how you can leverage online platforms to get in front of and connect with the Super Achievers.

Before going any further, I want you to honestly evaluate your progress so far. Have you consistently been taking action? Did you complete the homework tasks? Did you stick to your action goals that you set for yourself and achieve them by their deadlines? If not, it's worth going back and making sure that you have completed everything.

"When you knock on the door of opportunity, do not be surprised that it is Work who will answer" Brendon Burchard

Chapter Four: Networking on Social Media

"Behind every successful person, there are many successful relationships." Joe Applebaum

There are a lot of social media platforms out there and new ones are popping up every week. Different Super Achievers, leaders and influencers prefer different social media platforms based on the audience they are targeting. Most will have accounts on multiple social platforms. Instead of writing a 50,000-page book with exact specific strategies for each and every social media platform that exists, I am going to give you a general strategy that can be used by anyone, regardless of your level of competency with social media and adapted for virtually all social media platforms.

I am not going to discuss the advanced social media strategies as they can be quite complex and will take a lot of time to explain. Besides, I am not a social media expert. If you want to find out more and learn about them, then you are welcome to do you in your own time.

Furthermore, I can't give you strategies for social platforms of the future because I don't know what they will be as they don't even exist yet. However, you are smart, capable and resourceful enough to figure out how to adapt and apply these strategies to platforms that might be launched in the future.

This might be another learning curve because you might not be familiar with the social platforms where the Super Achievers of your choice are hanging out. Having said that, most social platforms are designed to be intuitive and simple to learn and use. YouTube and Google are your best friends here. Use them to learn more about the specific social platforms that you want to dominate.

Success is a slow process and it's also sequential. It requires you to align a series of events in a specific order over a period of time that will eventually lead you to your final goal. Like a domino run, you have to patiently put each piece into place carefully and then by applying the smallest of momentums to the right piece you can cause a chain reaction that is moving so fast that it can't be stopped until it's over.

Also, the bigger the impact you want to make, the more time, patience and pieces it requires. The illusion of 'overnight success' only exists because everyone only sees the majestic chain reaction of the domino run once it starts. No one sees the hours, days, weeks, months, years and sometimes decades that it took to set up all the pieces. These parallels between sequential success and dominoes were discussed by Gary Keller and Jay Papasan in their book 'The One Thing.'

The truth is that in every moment of our lives we have to make a decision to either lean a little bit towards creating our success or to lean a little bit towards complacency. Every moment counts because it's a moment that is lost forever. Therefore, it is up to us to decide whether we want to use that moment to set up more pieces for our success or adopt mediocrity as the new pinnacle.

"You are either moving forward or falling backwards. There is no standing still." Sayan Karmakar

I am not writing this so we can all hold hands, throw a pity party and cry away a box of tissues. I am writing this to highlight the fact that how you view your life and the value that you place on yourself, your dreams, your relationships and your success is what truly matters.

As I mentioned earlier, there are many social media platforms in existence and you might have to master multiple platforms to achieve your goals. However, based on my personal experience, the 2 main ones that yielded me the most success are Facebook and LinkedIn. Other people's experiences might be different, but I am basing this on my experience alone.

Facebook

Let's face it, everyone might not understand the difference between an asset and an investment, but everyone does have a Facebook account. (If you don't, it's time to climb out of your cave, ditch the clubs, get online and create one RIGHT NOW!!!) Facebook is one of the biggest and one of the most powerful social media platforms and it's a brilliant networking tool. Don't believe me? Check out this amazing article by Mark Schaefer, titled *"The Relational Power of Facebook for Business Networking"*[3]. In the article, he shares a story of a friend who avoided a massive strike from the workers and unions of a major manufacturing plant using Facebook, after all other channels of communications failed.

LinkedIn

LinkedIn is the biggest and the baddest professional networking platform in the world. This is where all the 'Big Guns' hang out. Unlike Facebook, which is designed to connect with friends and family, LinkedIn is specifically designed to connect the professionals of the world. You definitely need a LinkedIn

---

[3] https://businessesgrow.com/2017/07/31/facebook-for-business-networking/

profile and I personally do up to 80% of my networking on LinkedIn. I have had more success through LinkedIn than any other platform, including Facebook, Twitter, email, and Instagram. As a matter of fact, I am confident in making the claim that I have had more success via LinkedIn than all the other platforms combined!

Before we go any further, make sure that you have a LinkedIn account. If you don't, go to Linkedin.com and create one now. If you do have a LinkedIn account then you need to make sure that you have set up a professional-looking profile and all the information, and your profile picture, are up to date. If you are not sure how to set up a professional-looking profile, you can search for profiles of Super Achievers, on LinkedIn and have a look around. It's definitely worth investing the time to set up your profile properly, but don't worry about getting it absolutely perfect. Just go for the 85% solution. As long as it is complete and has all the main information there so you can start networking, then you are good to go. You can always come back and improve it later.

If you have never used Facebook or LinkedIn, or if you have only used them casually, then it's definitely worth investing some time to learn about how they both work and how you can get the most out of using them. There are lots of YouTube videos, blogs, articles and online courses from websites like Udemy.com and Skillshare.com, where you can go to learn more about Facebook, LinkedIn and other social media platforms.

TurboCharged Takeaways

➢ Take the time to invest in and learn about the different social media platforms where the Super Achievers on your list hang out.

➢ Make sure that your profile, your picture and your contact details are up-to-date.

➢ Facebook and LinkedIn are the 2 main social platforms to definitely focus on.

➢ Overnight success is an illusion. The real work happens when you spend hours, days, weeks, and years setting up the individual domino pieces before the domino run of your success starts.

In the next chapter, you will learn the strategy that you can adapt for any social media platform to find, connect and start the initial conversation with the super achievers.

Chapter Five: The Strategy for Social Media

"Networking is more about farming than it is about hunting. It is about cultivating relationships." Dr. Ivan Misner

Whilst everyone else goes on social media to catch up with their social lives and update their status 555 times a day, we are not going on there to locate local garage sales or to update our status after eating a blueberry muffin. We have a clear purpose with specific goals. Let's get started...

Locate the Target(s)

Click the search bar and type the name of the person who you are looking for. Find them and send a connection request. Not everyone will approve of your request straight away, so expect some delay. Some might never accept your request. Be OK with that, but don't give up because you can always send a follow-up message after your connection request. Remember, you are a stranger to them and they already get hundreds of requests every day. LinkedIn allows you to send a brief message, 300 characters long, along with your request to introduce yourself. It's optional, but I suggest that you make the most of it. Check the Swipe File – page viii for my examples.

Alternatively, you can find their business page and follow it and check out what's going on there. After following the page, you will start to get notifications in your news feed about the latest posts, etc.

Whether your connection request gets approved or you end up following their business page, keep an eye on the latest news. Are they writing a book? Are they attending an event, delivering a talk or a workshop? Who are they talking to right now? Knowing all this information will allow you to start a conversation, and the relationship, on a strong footing by demonstrating that you are genuinely interested in them and you have taken the time to research what is important to them.

Remember our 'Golden Rules' of being more interested than trying to be interesting yourself and curiosity? Michael Roderick suggests that when you reach out, mention where you came across their content and that you are curious about a certain point that they mentioned/talked about. Say that you know that they are really busy, but you were wondering if it would be possible to talk briefly to discuss that point further. It's a fantastic way to start a 'cold' conversation with someone who doesn't know you. This is precisely why it's so important to follow the Super Achievers on social media and familiarise yourself with their world.

A great way to catch the attention of the Super Achievers is to comment on their posts and the comments to their posts. Add value and share your best ideas. You can also share their posts on your profile or your page. If your name constantly appears on their news feed, they can see your comments adding value and they can see you sharing their posts, they will see you as a person of value.

By giving first in this way, you will demonstrate your position as someone who is truly a person of service. Most of the time the Super Achievers notice this and reach out to say 'Thank you!' This is a good time to start a conversation. If they don't reach out, then you can initiate a conversation by sending a message that mentions one of their posts that you found to be most interesting or inspiring with a short explanation of why.

A TurboCharged tip that I can share here is to record a video message instead of a written message to really stand out.

Join the Communities

Many social media sites like Facebook and LinkedIn also allow like-minded people to create a group/community where they can interact and share ideas about their area of interest. Find out if the people on your list belong to any groups or communities and join them. Some groups are free to join, while others are paid. Some you can join with a click of a button and some are private and require you to send a joining request which has to be approved by the group's administrator(s). Make sure that you read the 'Rules' that all members of the group(s) have to abide by. Mostly, it's standard stuff like no swearing, respect for others, no self-promotions, etc., etc. Your job is to follow them religiously, regardless of what others are doing.

Also, make sure to introduce yourself to the group/community. It is critical that you do introduce yourself to everyone because unless you do, no one is going to know who you are and what you are working on. You can't network from the sidelines, people!

Your introduction will be the first contact that people will have with you and you definitely want to make a spellbinding first impression. I am sharing with you an example of the message that I have used, which you are welcome to adapt and use. Use the link on "Before You Read" - page viii to download the pdf file.

Otherwise, feel free to create your own version. Just make sure that you cover all the main areas, such as your name (duh!), what main project you are working on, why is it important to you, how you plan to help others accelerate their lives and what kind of people are you currently trying to surround yourself with.

You also need to actively participate in the group/community. That means making sure that you are staying up-to-date with the latest posts and initiatives that are launched. Come from a place of giving and contribute as much as you can. You will be surrounded by other like-minded people who are on a similar journey to yours and so by contributing to the community and helping others you can quickly establish yourself as a person of high value. You will start to see a spike in the number of people interacting with you and responding to your posts and replies. You want to get to a place where people are coming to you with their questions. That's when you can really make an impact.

Moreover, all this activity and value will be noticed by the Super Achievers in there because every time they will open their page, they will see your name and the value that you are bringing to the community.

This is really powerful because there are probably going to be hundreds or thousands of people who are members, but never actually contribute to the community. They just sit on the sidelines, leaving the court open for power players like you to Super Hero your way to Awesomeness. (Yes, this is technical jargon. I literally just created it) It might seem like a really big step to put yourself out there, potentially attracting everyone's judgement, but if you want to win big, then you will have to play big. Comfort zones are for marshmallows!

By following these exact steps, I have been able to secure world-class mentors, make new friends all over the world, gain access to new opportunities that I would not have been able to gain otherwise and get amazing advice for absolutely free. Did it take time, effort and patience? You know it did. Were the results absolutely worth it? Heck yeah!

I found a time during the day when I would be able to sit down and complete the daily networking tasks on Facebook and then scheduled it into my phone's calendar. I love phone calendars by the way. It's super convenient to just put everything into it and forget about it. When the time comes it automatically reminds me. I don't need to worry about remembering everything all the time, whilst I'm hitting life at 10,000 miles an hour and I don't need to run around trying to remember where I last saw my diary or planner. It's automatic and I can stay on top of it all like clockwork. I almost always have my phone with or near me, wherever I am. I charge it every night and I have all the important social apps installed so I don't need to login to my laptop every time. I can work from wherever I am. Most of the time I just use Google Assistant and dictate all the reminders, meetings and To-Dos. I would advise you to use your phone's calendar and its digital assistant to their maximum capabilities.

Another great advantage of joining groups and communities is that they usually run in-house initiatives such as book clubs, mentoring support, virtual events, guest interviews and featuring their members, just to name a few. These initiatives are a great opportunity for you to actively get involved and gain recognition quickly. But remember, you have to add value to others first before you can have any expectations about them adding value to you.

If you successfully launch the conversations with the Super Achievers and others in the groups, then it's time to put what we have covered so far into practice. Ask the 'Magic Question', be curious about what they said or are working on, follow the

'Golden Rules' and add value to them. Invest in and build those relationships.

There will also be times when you discover a problem that you can help to solve, a resource that you can share that will massively add value to the Super Achiever or the community, a personal connection that you can make with someone who can resolve their issues or a question that you can answer. In such a case, you do not need to ask the 'Magic Question' to discover their pain points, instead, you can put together a proposal to present to them to help them solve the issue.

This can be extremely powerful as you don't need to go through the process of discovery, but instead, you can start by adding value right off the beginning. Just make sure your proposal is clear, strong and concise. You want to make a good impression so that they are at least willing to have a conversation about it.

During the conversation, don't talk about all your previous accomplishments and minimize the technical jargon. You do not need to impress them. If they weren't impressed, they wouldn't be talking to you. Instead, answer their questions, be confident and reassuring and clearly explain exactly how you can help.

Don't make promises you can't keep and agree on a deadline that is convenient for everyone. When it's time for action, follow through by the deadline or before and overdeliver the value. My advice is to agree on a deadline that is a little longer than you actually need. When you deliver before the time that they are expecting it to be finished, you will instantly achieve Rock Star status. They will see you as a person of value and will want to work with you again.

In summary, keep your eyes peeled when on social media for any opportunities to add value.

I want you to succeed. I want you to win. I want you to TurboCharge your life. This is why I am doing all the hard work for you. Not only am I giving you all the strategies in granular detail, but I am also giving you examples of messages and reviews that I have written myself for writing your message and introductions so you don't have to spend any time, energy, or effort trying to figure this stuff out for yourself. You can get them from the link on "Before You Read" - page viii.

I am doing all this hard work so you can just focus on taking action. That's where all the results are and I want to make it as easy as possible for you to initiate the action.

"Action cures fear, inaction creates terror." Douglas Horton

TurboCharged Takeaways

➤ Find the Super Achievers on your list on social media and send a friend request, or follow their business page.

➤ Join any groups and communities that the Super Achievers have also joined.

➤ Actively participate, follow the 'Golden Rules' and add value.

➤ Use my templates to initiate contact with the Super Achievers and introduce yourself to any groups/communities

➤ Use your phone' calendar and digital assistant to your advantage

➤ Take Action!!!

PART III: Events

In Part 2 we covered the strategy for using social media to find, connect and start the initial conversation with the Super Achievers. Now, in Part 3, we are going to cover the networking strategies for events: formal, informal and virtual. The advantages of attending physical events are many, however, one of the main benefits is that lots of Super Achievers are all present at the same physical place. You can approach them directly, instead of sending a connection request, waiting for it to be accepted and then starting a conversation.

Moreover, at physical events, the Super Achievers are already expecting to meet lots of new people and are therefore more likely to be willing to talk.

At the time of writing this book in 2020/2021, virtual events are becoming more and more popular, thanks to COVID-19 aka Coronavirus aka pain-in-everyone's (insert appropriate body part).

Even though you might not be able to meet with the Super Achievers in person face-to-face, you can still employ what you have learnt so far, and other strategies that I will share with you, to connect with the Super Achievers.

Talking to a Super Achiever in real life does take a certain level of courage and confidence. We develop confidence, over time, when we act courageously, despite the presence of risk and fear. The fact is that in order to act courageously and develop confidence we need to have a strong bias towards taking action; a firm theme throughout this book and something I believe in, to my very core. We will have to remind ourselves, in moments of doubt, that we are Big Boys and Big Girls, smile, and start a conversation with them.

"Confidence is your reward for overcoming fears."
Anonymous quote

Chapter Six: Formal Events

"It's not what you know or who you know, it's who knows you."
Susan RoAne

Formal events are conferences, meetings, presentations, trainings, workshops, etc. They have a clear structure and an agenda. There will probably be guest speakers delivering at the event and you will probably have to purchase tickets to attend the event.

Most people believe that the most important thing to gain from these events is the content. I respectfully disagree. While the content indeed is important, however, the most important thing to gain from these events are actually the contacts that you can develop and the relationships that you can build. Content is limiting. Instead, you can gain limitless potential by connecting with the actual people who are delivering the content. The content they deliver is a very small part of their knowledge, skills, experience and expertise. It's infinitely more valuable to go to the source of the content, the Super Achievers themselves, and build relationships with them.

Pre-Event Actions

Before the event, get a hold of the agenda and the list of people delivering presentations, talks, or workshops. Do some research and find out who they all are. You might be familiar with some, but it's still good to go online and find out what they have been up to lately. Get on social media, follow them and connect with them. It's going to be super powerful if you have connected with them online before the event because unlike everyone else at the event, they will know who you are when you go there. It really strengthens your position when you actually speak to them in person.

Once they accept your connection request, ask the 'Magic' question and offer to help. Use the link on "Before You Read" - page viii to get examples of messages that I have used to help you write your own, but the angle you want to take here is that you know they are going to this big event and so are you and you are very excited to meet them. However, you realise that they are very busy and you are wondering if there is anything you can do to help them prepare for the event.

Some might not respond, or not need your help. However, that's not the point. The point is to get in front of them before the actual event so that they are familiar with who you are. In the message, you can very briefly introduce yourself and what you are working on. Now you can go to the event with the confidence that you have already 'broken the ice' with them at a basic level.

If someone does tell you what they need help with, then try to find a way to help them. Trust me, you are probably going to be the only person ever who helped them with something before one of their big days and as a reward, you will gain instant value in their eyes.

In Dec 2016, I attended a personal development event in London and I used this exact strategy where I had found the list of the guest speakers, a.k.a. Super Achievers, and I reached out to all of them before the event on social media to offer my help. Even though not everyone responded back to me, I ended up having great conversations and forming connections with some of the Super Achievers who did respond back. When I arrived at the event it was so easy for me to walk up to each of them as they immediately recognised me, smiled, and addressed me by my name. It was a completely different reaction to how they were meeting, greeting and talking with the other attendees. It was also different for me because I felt completely comfortable approaching them as if I was meeting a friend. Furthermore, since they already knew me and were aware of what I was working on, they were happy to introduce me to other Super Achievers at the event, even those who hadn't responded to me on social media. In the end, I gained some amazing new connections and even booked some for interviews on my YouTube channel. Bottom line: It works. Do it!

Plan the travel and book any train tickets etc. in advance. Make sure you know the route to the venue well. If you are driving, call the venue and book a parking spot for yourself in advance or find out where the nearest affordable parking is available. Overnight stay also needs to be planned and booked if you are travelling far. If the food is not provided at the event, prepare your own lunch. You want to get the most from your time there so a quick 10 min sandwich break means that you can spend the rest of lunchtime getting in front of more people. While most people will leave the venue and go out for lunch etc. You want to stay there and connect with others.

Pick out the clothes you are going to wear. Make sure that you dress well. You want to look the part. I don't mean that you wear flashy clothes and draw inappropriate attention to yourself. Wear good, clean smart clothes. My tip is to dress up rather than dressing down. It's better to be a little bit overdressed, rather than being underdressed. It's also ok to look stylish and have a fresh unique look, but it's definitely not ok to dress like a mannequin that belongs in the window of a shop that specializes in 70s disco wear. You want to look more 'put together' than everyone else there. Another element to this is to ensure that your grooming game is in top shape.

Gentlemen! Nose hair. Ear hair. Neck hair. Back hair. Haircut. Trim the beard. Underarm hair. Mints. Get it all under control! (Yeah, I just went there. Deal with it!) For world-class grooming and style tips check out Aaron Marino. In this entire world, I listen to him and him alone.[4]

Ladies! I'm not going to say much here. You guys know what to do. Just remember that it's a networking event, not a beauty pageant. You do not need to look like a catwalk model. Dress smart, dress sharp, dress with style. Just control the makeup, jewelry, (inset ridiculous number) inch heels and the party clothes.

The best way I can describe the look that I go for when I attend an event is that I want to look like a smartly dressed savage.

Next, regardless of your gender, wear a scent. Any room, no matter how big, feels small when there are a lot of people packed in. We can take total advantage of this and use a fresh scent to immediately stand out. That's usually the last thing on everyone's mind. Trust me, if you are smartly dressed, well-groomed, are always smiling and smell like a million Pounds (British Sterling baby!) no one will forget you.

By the way, you don't need to carry the bulky bottle of scent with you the whole time, just transfer your scent into a small refillable bottle and take that with you so you can top up throughout the whole day. If you don't have one, you can pick them up super cheaply from somewhere like Amazon. They are

---

[4] Aaron Marino's website: https://iamalpham.com/
Aaron's YouTube channel: https://bit.ly/3rmwoOm

refillable reusable travel bottles that are discreet and small; about the size of your pinky finger.

Just think about how you would dress, smell and look if you were going to meet the parents of the person of your dreams for the first time. The family of your one true love, your fantastical fairytale bliss.

Practice your intro. How you introduce yourself to someone is going to be a huge part of you making a spellbinding first impression. It's going to be like your elevator pitch, with a 10-second window. At this stage, all that hard work that you put in earlier on social media will pay off. If the person whom you are meeting has already communicated with you via social media, then use it to your advantage. Here are some examples:

Whilst shaking hands *

"Hi (name of the Super Achiever). I am (your name). We met on (name of social media platform). It's a pleasure to finally meet you. What has been the most exciting part of your day so far?"

If the person did not respond to you then try this:

Whilst shaking hands*

"Hi (name of Super Achiever). I am (your name). I have been inspired by your work, especially by (mention something that you found inspiring on the social feed) that you posted about on (name of the social platform). I want to clarify/I am curious about what you said in your (mention social media post/article/interview)

You can practice this, either with someone who can give you feedback or at least use a mirror to evaluate yourself. You want this to be a pleasant interaction and you want things to flow naturally.

It would also be useful to take a small pad and a pen to take notes after each interaction. You can quickly write down contact details, ideas and all the people you are going to follow up with after the event. From my experience, it's good to write things down as you go along. You will be meeting a lot of people in a small amount of time and it would be very difficult to remember what everyone said and what you said to them, at the end of the day. Best to write it down immediately.

On the other hand, also prepare some questions for each of the speakers beforehand so that you don't have to think of the questions on the spot. Before attending the event is the perfect opportunity to take all the time you need to think of and prepare high-value questions that you are going to ask the Super Achievers and steal the show.

Charge your phone, tablet, camera, dictaphone, etc. Take extra batteries and a battery pack with you. Make sure that everything is working and has enough memory for photos, videos and audio recordings. Always ask permission before you take photos, selfies or record anything. However, don't make that the main focus. Remember, it's about building relationships, not about updating your social accounts and phone memory with epic selfies.

Is that the doorbell? Oh look, it's the postman with a sharply wrapped package for you, must be that fresh layer of confidence that you ordered. Go on, try it on. Oh yeah! That's what I'm talking about. In this case, confidence will come through your preparation. If you have been following everything in the book so far, you are super prepared to go to any event and crush your networking goals like a boss!

Finally, don't forget that gorgeous smile at home.

During the Event

Arrive early. Secure/locate your seat. Make sure that it's at the end of the row and not in the middle where it would be difficult for you to get out and move around. After arriving, make sure that you actually talk to the people there, instead of checking your phone. Test all your equipment, check the batteries and the memory.

Next, locate the toilets so that you know where to go and you don't get lost. This is also a great opportunity to freshen up and top-up that mint and scent.

Participate in the activities, workshops, etc. Take notes about what each of the speakers mentioned so that when you speak with them, you can refresh your memory quickly with the main points.

After their talk, presentation or workshop finishes they usually allow time for any questions from the audience. If not, just raise your hand anyway because what I am going to share with you next is another 'networking goldmine' of a trick.

When the opportunity for the questions usually comes most people shy away and don't ask any questions because they don't want to draw attention to themselves, or they don't have any questions prepared and so they are at a loss at the moment about what to ask. If you have followed my advice and pre-prepared some questions and you have been taking notes, then hopefully, you will have at least 1 great question that you can ask. I want you to jump on this opportunity to ask questions like a drowning sea-wrecked person would jump on a luxury yacht with a free 24/7 Turkish buffet. However, instead of asking your question just like everyone else, you are going to take a more structured and purposeful approach.

Here's how most people ask questions:

"Hi. Thanks for being here. I just wanted to ask...."

There is no clear structure to this and it's a complete waste of a phenomenal opportunity.

Here's how you are going to ask your question:

"Hi (insert name of Super Achiever). I am (insert your name). I am (mention what you do). Currently, I am (mention your current goal and what kind of people you want to surround yourself with.) Thank you so much for being here. You added a tremendous amount of value to me and to all of us here. I really loved your talk/presentation/speech, especially what you said about (pick an interesting point from your notes.) My question to you is: (ask the question)"

Not only have you asked the question, but you did it clearly and you just introduced yourself to the whole room and told everyone what you do and what you are working to achieve. Now people who resonate with what you said will automatically tune in and will be itching to seek you out and connect with you throughout the whole day. You have literally reduced your networking effort by almost 75% because you don't have to chase all the people there and try to gain more connections. Instead, everyone there will be aching to chase and grab a hold of you.

When you ask the question, all eyes are on you and you are in the spotlight. By introducing yourself to the entire audience in one go you are essentially giving everyone an open invitation to come and speak to you. You are the proverbial flame and everyone else is a metaphorical moth.

Another great time to catch the Super Achievers and start a conversation is when they have finished their presentation/talk etc. and they are walking off the stage. This is where sitting close to the front and at the end of a row pays off. You can quickly run up to them without interrupting anyone and strike that conversation. You can do this at the end of every talk or presentation. Whilst everyone else is busy clapping, get your butt out of your seat and run to them before they disappear. There wouldn't be a queue for you to navigate. Come on people, where is your sense of urgency?!

Your goal should be to get their details instead of giving them your business card or contact details. Everyone else there is going to try and give them their business card and the Super Achiever is not going to remember who was who by the end of the event. They are probably going to think about throwing them all in the bin, but then feel guilty about it and put them in the recycling instead. Differentiate yourself from the herd.

I know it's tempting, but try to control yourself with the pictures and the selfies. Once again, everyone else there is going to ask them for a picture or a selfie and so if you don't want the Super Achievers to see you like everyone else, then control yourself. You want them to see you as a person of value and their equal, instead of another selfie junkie.

Take a few extra bottles of water with you, obviously for yourself, but also because oftentimes an opportunity presents itself for you to instantly stand out from the crowd. Usually, at the event, the Super Achievers are delivering a talk or presenting one after another and so they have a tight schedule. During their presentation, they realise that they are thirsty or their throat is getting dry and they need some water and quite often the organisers forget to provide water for the speakers. At this point, they would ask the organisers of the event to get them some water and you just struck pure gold! Whilst, everyone starts panicking and fumbling around to try and locate a source of water, grab that spare bottle of water, run up to the stage and hand it to them. Everyone has just witnessed your greatness, especially that Super Achiever who is going to be extremely grateful and will be happy to make your acquaintance as you grab them when they come off the stage after finishing their presentation.

When connecting with other attendees, it is ok to give them your business card and to get their business cards in return. Again, I find it useful to take brief notes on the business card itself to help me remember the conversation with each person and any commitments that I made to help them. If you are not sure how to meet other attendees then try this: "Hey, what's your story?"

Asking an open question like the one above means that the other person has the choice to answer however they want and it gives you the opportunity to learn more about them. The single most important key to any conversation is to *listen carefully and to show genuine interest in what the other person is saying.* Since everyone likes talking about themselves, this is the perfect question to nudge them in the right direction. Alternatively, start the conversation by giving them a compliment like, "Love your watch! You have great taste. What made you buy it?"

Be genuinely curious and find out more about them, then ask the 'Magic' question and offer to help. If you see alignment between the two of you, then exchange business cards and/or contact details.

Talk to as many people as you can and don't forget to talk to the organisers, staff and volunteers. You never know how someone will prove themselves to be useful. Most of the time, they all get ignored by everyone, when in fact, they usually know and have access to all the Super Achievers that everyone else is there to meet. By meeting and connecting with them you are essentially traveling through a wormhole to shortcut your way to the Super Achievers.

You want to use your time effectively and connect with as many people as possible because like we talked about earlier, "Every problem is a people problem" and "Every goal is a people goal". Therefore, the more people you meet the higher the chances that you will meet the right people for you.

Don't get me wrong, I am not saying that you have to talk to every single person there. That would be both impossible and exhausting. What I am trying to say is that by talking to lots of people you are drastically improving your chances of finding the people whom you are searching for.

You need to look at the situation with a wider lens. Each person is a gateway into a new world full of new people, ideas, knowledge, resources, technology, money, and opportunities. It's not just the person in front of you, it's about everything and everyone that they know too. All you have to do is share what you need help with and what type of people you want to surround yourself with. A great opportunity to talk about this is when the other person is trying to get to know more about you and asks something like, *"So, what do you do?" "Tell me about yourself..." "What are you all about?"* If you have shown genuine interest in the other person first, they would naturally want to know more about you.

If you go to the event with a friend or a group of people whom you know; don't stay with them all the time. Make sure to go around and mingle with other people. You want to use this tremendous opportunity to boost your network. It is easy and comfortable to always talk to the same people, sit with them, eat with them, etc. But you must make yourself available for everyone else too. Briefly see your friends and say that you will connect with them a bit later. Then, scan the battlefield and get ready for action.

At this point, I want to highlight the fact that the dedication and authenticity with which you will meet the Super Achievers also extends to everyone else too. You cannot have 2 different standards for different types of people. You are always 'selling yourself' and everyone else is watching. This is why you must always 'sell yourself' to the same exquisite standard, regardless of who you are dealing with. All the 'Golden Rules' that we covered before still apply. You must show the same level of commitment and dedication to one and all and try to add value to them. Hold yourself to the highest standards, always!

"We are what we repeatedly do. Excellence, then, is not an act, but a habit." Aristotle

Post Event Actions

Hopefully, you have now secured lots of new contacts, expanded your network, started new friendships and have connected with many Super Achievers. It's now time for housekeeping, following up and fulfilling any commitments that you made.

After the event, you need to contact everyone that you met, Super Achiever or not, and send them a message. Here, the notes that you took throughout the day will prove to be extremely useful. You need to follow up with everyone that you met. Ideally, you want to do this within the first 24 hours after the event. You will probably be the only one who follows up with them so quickly.

If you met someone new at the event, regardless of whether they were a Super Achiever, an attendee, or support staff, make sure that you come home and research them. Follow them on social media, find out what's happening in their news feed, ask the 'Magic' question, offer to help, add value and fulfil any commitments that you made e.g., sending an article, sharing a resource, or making an introduction. Also, it helps save all their contact details in a spreadsheet so that you always have everyone's details saved in one place for easy access. You don't need anything fancy here. Just a simple spreadsheet that you can use to track your networking contacts would do.

Homework

There you have it. Your plan for savagely networking at formal events. So, go ahead, get online and research the events that you are interested in. When you find something that you want and are able to attend, make the booking. Then follow the plan and then witness your networking game go from like a 3.8 to a 13.5!

Action Deadline

"I am committed to…

_____

_____

_____

_____

_____

_____

Therefore, by _____ I will have

completed all my homework.

TurboCharged Takeaways

➢ Before the event, do all your research and prep. Don't leave anything to chance.

➢ Use social to connect with the Super Achievers, ask the 'Magic' question, offer your help and add value.

➢ At the event ask questions purposefully using the structure that I shared with you.

➢ After their presentation, as a Super achiever is leaving the stage, run up to them and start a conversation.

➢ Connect with other attendees and take notes.

➢ Reach out and send individual messages to everyone that you met at the event within 24 hours after the event.

➢ Save everyone's contact details in a spreadsheet.

In the next chapter, we are going to break down the plan for attending informal events.

Chapter Seven: Informal Events

"Networking is an enrichment program, not an entitlement program." Susan RoAne

Informal events are usually much smaller than formal events and are usually set in an informal setting such as a café, a park, a local village hall, etc. with only a small collection of people in attendance. Sometimes they are held regularly for people to attend. You can identify informal events from their scale and their toned-down nature. These usually tend to be breakfast meetups, coffee mornings, lunch gatherings, etc. with networking opportunities and maybe 1 or 2 educational elements such as expert presentations or interviews. You can probably find some of these in your local area. Some might charge a small fee.

You are probably not going to find any typical Super Achievers at these events (top experts, leaders, and influencers); however, you can probably connect with people who are ahead of you and who can show you the next few steps to help you accelerate. It would definitely be beneficial to get feedback from others on what you are working on and get some new ideas, resources and systems from them. If something is working for someone else, it's definitely worth a try.

Here you can practice, gain confidence, hone your skills and gain momentum. You can meet other like-minded people and expand your immediate network which you can leverage to win at a higher level. We will talk about the power of, and the strategies for, leveraging your network a bit later.

Just like formal events that we looked at in the last chapter, the most important thing about these events is not the content that is being covered, it's the people. Unlike formal events, informal events are more enabling when it comes to building relationships. This is because these events are usually held quite regularly and are attended by mostly the same people. Since you are going to see the same people it's a lot easier to get to know them.

Using very broad, emphasis on 'very' and 'broad', brushstrokes I am going to split informal events into 3 main categories:

➢ Meeting groups – events organised for people with similar interests

➢ Networking groups – these exist to help people connect with new people to build their contacts

➢ Masterminds – you can join these to get peer mentoring, advice and support to solve your problems

Some might be free to join and attend, while others might have a fee. Inquire about the financial commitments before so you are clear on what to expect. As I said before, the most important thing about any event is the contacts and the relationships that you build there, not the content. Again, just because it's not a formal event and the people who you might meet here are not the typical 'Super Achievers', doesn't mean that we can slack. Remember the 'Golden Rules' and the 'Magic' question. Service comes first, always!

Pre-Event Actions

Who is the most important person at these events? No, it's not your weird uncle Barry who turns up at almost everything uninvited, it's the organisers. They will probably know everyone and will have everyone's trust and contact details, therefore, connecting with them and forming a relationship will be like creating your own networking wormhole.

Before the event, find out who the organisers are and do some research online. Connect with them on social media, introduce yourself and offer your help. Even though they haven't met you yet, they will appreciate you reaching out to them and introducing yourself. Also, they will see you as someone who is mature, responsible and as a person of value who they would be happy to have at the event and expose to their network.

Doing this is also greatly beneficial because when you go to the event, not only will you be able to greet the organisers personally because they already know you, but also because instead of trying to hunt down the ideal people to connect with, you can just approach the organisers and ask them to introduce you to the people who fit your desired profile. Here's what it could look like:

"Hey (name of organiser). Thanks for having me today. Since I am new and I don't know anyone, I was wondering if you wouldn't mind introducing me to some people. Currently, I am looking to surround myself with (mention the type of people you want to connect with)."

During the Event

Dress smart. Like we discussed before, it's better to be a little overdressed, rather than being underdressed. You don't need to dress up to the same extent as when you attend a formal event, but first impressions count, so no slacking! You still want to make a spellbinding first impression. Also, don't forget that scent.

Arrive early. This is one of those unbreakable commandments. There is no escaping this. Arriving early will also allow you to see people as they arrive and start networking with them.

Don't hound them as soon as they walk in. Give them some time to get their bearings and get settled. Before everyone has to sit down and the event actually starts, it's a great opportunity to mingle. Introduce yourself, use your elevator pitch. Hopefully, the few people you meet at the start will have you at the front of their mind and they will introduce you to others they know during the rest of the event without you having to put in any extra effort. It's a good idea to stay within their line of sight.

During an online networking group, I connected with (let's call her Tina). Tina was an Image Consultant who helps busy professionals to transform their image on and off-screen to make a great first impression. Tina and I met on a separate call after the meeting and she asked me to share some networking strategies to get more clients. I asked her to give me her intro and elevator pitch as if I was a potential client. She did a great job of describing what she did, however, it required multiple sentences, and at the end, I didn't feel excited and it didn't make me curious to find out more.

I believe that your title and your elevator pitch need to do more than just introduce yourself and tell the other person what you do. I believe that your title and your elevator pitch need to *be unique, engage the other person emotionally,* and *pique their curiosity* so that they are excited and keen to find out more about you and your work, instead of you talking at them to try and get them interested.

I helped Tina refine her title and elevator pitch so it was something close to, "I am an Image Confidence Coach and I help busy professionals to gain the confidence they need to crush it in life and in business." I then tasked Tina with sharing her new title and elevator pitch every chance she got. 2 days later I got an email from Tina informing me that she has a booking call with someone whom she had met previously, but didn't click at the time, after she used her new elevator pitch. Such is the power of a strong elevator pitch. Feel free to use this example as a template to craft your elevator pitch.

Just be aware that having a killer elevator pitch is not enough, how you deliver it also matters. I would highly encourage you to practice so you sound confident and natural, rather than sounding like you are reading it from a brochure or sounding robotic

Let's take this to the Ultimate Networking Warrior Ninja level. During a physical gathering, arriving late means you get whichever seat is free. Arriving early, on the other hand, allows you to choose where you sit. You want to pick a seat that has a clear view of the door so you can see who is leaving and who is still present. You also want to maximise your view of the venue. From your seat, you should be able to see the whole room/hall/office so you know what is happening at all times and you can track the movement of people throughout the event. I can't give a 'Golden Rule' with a 'One Solution Fits All' answer since each location will be different with a unique layout, but keep these things in mind when you are choosing a seat.

A great tip to follow here is to try to have your back to the wall. That way you don't have anyone sitting behind you and you can scan the whole room with one glance. Obviously, you want to make sure that you still have mobility so you can move around. If it's a choice between mobility and visibility, I would recommend sacrificing visibility for mobility. You can always move around and get a better view, but if you are boxed in, you can't move around and approach people even if you can see them.

Bring something to take notes with and also bring business cards. It's absolutely fine to hand out business cards at informal events, however, it is still recommended to get the other person's contact details instead of giving them your contact details. One strategy that I used to employ pre-Covid all the time was to get to the 'Add New Contact' screen on my phone and asked them for their contact details, including their phone, number, email address, website, etc. and then added them as a new contact to the category/group named after the event I met them at. On the 'Add New Contact' screen, under the 'Notes' section, I added the date of the event and any other brief notes such as how I was introduced to them, their business or occupation, and whom I want to connect them with, etc.

Sometimes at informal events, you might be asked to introduce yourself to the group, if so, grab that chance like your life depends on it. You can use the elevator pitch that you devised earlier with a brief description. Here's what it can look like:

"Hi everyone. (Insert your elevator pitch). Currently, I am (mention what is your goal and what kind of people you want to surround yourself with.) I would love to hear your thoughts and ideas on how I can get there. I promise you I wouldn't bite unless you are my dentist. (Insert short laugh) Thank you so much for having me."

Humour is good here as it 'breaks-the-ice' and makes people remember you for the joke you told when you were introducing yourself.

During breaks and networking sessions, scan the room and identify 'key zones' where people seem unsure about what to do next or a looking for someone familiar to go. In her exceptional book *'Captivate'* Vanessa Van Edwards calls these key zones *"Hotspots"* and suggests that they are likely to be after people have got themselves a drink and/or food and are looking around to find somewhere to go or someone to talk to. Seize the moment and approach them with a conversation starter like, *"Did you also go for the spring rolls?" "Ah, a fellow coffee lover. Now I don't have to feel alone!"*

These *"Hotspots"* can also occur when people are sitting down to eat/drink. You might spot someone sitting by themselves. You can be their savior and approach them with a big smile and ask, *"Is it ok if I join you?"* After they answer in the affirmative, you can follow up with something like, *"So, what brings you here?"* They will probably spend the rest of the time secretly thanking you for saving them.

If you want to join a group of people who are already engaged in a conversation, a great way to enter into the conversation without being a random-lingering-creepy-person is to say something like, *"Hi guys! Sorry, I just came here. What are we all talking about?"*

Post Event Actions

Here, the advice is the same as it was for formal events in the last chapter. Follow through and fulfil all your commitments. Reach out and send a short 'Thank You' message to everyone you met at the event, including the organisers, ideally within 24 hours of the event. Follow all the new people on social and make the connection like we have talked about. Establish yourself as a person of value to everyone.

Homework

Alright, now it's time to execute! Go online and find out about the events happening in your local area and attend them. Life happens when you take action, so stop holding back. Go all out. Execute!

Action Deadline

"I am committed to…

_____

_____

_____

_____

_____

_____

_____

Therefore, by _____ I will have

completed all my homework.

TurboCharged Takeaways

➤ Informal events take place regularly and are mostly attended by the same people

➤ The organisers are probably the most important people to connect with. Take the time to form a relationship with them

➤ Dress smart, arrive early and sit strategically.

➤ If the opportunity presents itself, introduce yourself to everyone

➤ Get the other person's contact details, instead of just handing out your business card

➤ After the event, follow up with all the commitments that you made and make sure to come from a place of value.

In the next chapter, you will learn how to network during virtual events.

Chapter Eight: Virtual Events

"The currency of real networking is not greed, but generosity."
Keith Ferrazzi

Virtual events are online conferences, webinars and virtual summits, as well as, online groups that meet regularly. Most of these are held over Zoom. Their popularity has been increasing due to the ease of access and low organizing costs and time commitments. However, in a COVID-19 afflicted world, these virtual events are becoming increasingly popular. I certainly have noticed a massive increase in the number of virtual and online events since the arrival of Coronavirus. They seem to be everywhere. I have had multiple invites to attend events that are happening live at the same time on the same day and I have had to clearly prioritise which ones I want to attend.

Pre-Event Actions

The initial part of the strategy is going to be the same as for attending physical events:

➢ Before the event, get a hold of the agenda and the list of people delivering presentations, talks, or workshops. The great news is that most virtual event organisers make the list of the guest attendees available to everyone days before the actual conference. You can use this list to identify your networking targets. Get on social media, follow them and connect with them.

➢ Ask the 'Magic' question and offer to help. Offer your services and ask if there is anything you can do to help them prepare for the event.

➤ If someone does tell you what they need help with, then try to find a way to help them.

➤ Prepare some interesting questions to ask each speaker/presenter.

Additional preparation for online events involves:

➤ Ensure that you have a good internet connection. Ideally, connect your PC/laptop with the ethernet cable instead of just using Wi-Fi to ensure a more stable connection.

➤ If you are going to be using video during the event, don't rely on your PC/laptop/s built-in webcam. Instead, get a HD webcam, especially since more and more events are likely to happen online due to the global pandemic. Also, dress smart. People are going to be watching you.

➤ If you do not have a suitable backdrop behind you, then most online platforms like Zoom now have the option of blurred or virtual backgrounds, but use them with caution as they are not always stable and movement can lead to a distorted image.

➤ Ensure that there is suitable lighting, especially if you are attending the event at night. You don't want to look washed out, but you also do not want to have too many shadows. I suggest using multiple light sources to balance the light and avoid shadows. Another option is to get a Ring Light, which are popular with many vloggers and models to achieve a healthy light balance. I use a clip-on ring light with my laptop that I picked up for a reasonable price on Amazon. It plugs into the USB slot on my laptop and has the controls to change the brightness, light modes (White, Natural or Warm) and to turn it on/off. I can also change the angle of the light with 360° rotation controls. Most importantly, it's compact, lightweight, and portable.[5] During the daytime, face the window instead of facing away from it.

➢ Find a quiet place without any distractions and background noise.

➢ Use a notepad a pen to jot down the main points and notes to follow-up later or for future reference

➢ Test the link/access details to make sure that they work. If not, contact the organisers immediately.

➢ Ensure that your social profiles are up-to-date and that you have a professional online identity e.g., don't use an old unprofessional, or hilarious, email address.

➢ Make sure that you have prepared and practiced your elevator pitch for introductions and breakout rooms. Elevator

During the Event

Virtual events offer an excellent opportunity to stay visible throughout the event by participating in discussions, actively commenting and responding to other's comments, asking questions and engaging in breakout sessions. Your comments and questions should be thoughtful and thought-provoking to spark conversations. Openly sharing your ideas and insights is a great way to demonstrate your expertise and build authority, which will position you as a person of influence and attract immediate attention. However, make sure not to appear as a

---

[5]

https://www.amazon.co.uk/gp/product/B08YRG93RS/ref=ppx_yo_dt_b_a sin_title_o00_s00?ie=UTF8&psc=1

spammer. Allow others to comment, share ideas and ask their questions too.

You should also use the private chat function, if it is available, to engage with other attendees as, unlike physical events, virtual events do not usually have restrictions on private conversations during the talks and presentations. You can use these conversations to build new contacts throughout the event. To get the dialogue flowing I recommend asking the other person about their opinion on the speaker/presentation. However, don't bombard them with questions or continuously disturb them with messages. Follow the pace that they set so that they feel comfortable and are happy to continue the conversation.

Enter the contact details of any new contacts into a document or spreadsheet to contact them later and prioritise them in the order of importance or urgency. You can categorise your connections into different groups. For example, you can set your 3 categories as below:

➢ People you have a reason to connect with immediately

➢ People who you want to build a deep relationship with

➢ People who you want to keep on your radar, but you do not need to connect with right now

Prioritising your contacts gives you a clear plan of action to follow after the event.

In case of virtual events, the hosts usually ask people to add their contact details in the chat, so all you have to do is to make sure that you save the chat before the meeting ends. Afterwards, you can filter through the saved chat with the help of your notes to find the key people you want to connect with and any follow-up actions that you need to carry out.

Post Event Actions

Follow up with your connections from the virtual event afterwards, ideally within 24 hours of the event. 24 hours is a good rule to follow because the conversations and discussions that you have had are still fresh in everyone's minds. Thank them for their ideas and insights and fulfil any commitments that you have made e.g., sending links, sharing resources and making introductions.

It's not always possible to connect with the Super Achievers at the virtual events as they usually have another presentation to deliver at a different event straight afterwards and they rush off as quickly as they get a chance. However, before leaving they share their contact details and where people can go to connect with them. Make sure that you capture those details as soon as they appear on the screen.

One way that I have found to be extremely effective is to capture a screenshot of the screen and save it. You can do it on computers and laptops by using the 'prt sc' button or by using the 'Snipping Tool'. On tablets and smartphones, you can use the default button combination (it's different for different phones) to capture screenshots, or otherwise, you can download specific apps to record or capture your screen. I have an Android phone and I use Screen Master (I have no affiliation with Screen Master. I just think it's a brilliant app!) to capture my phone screen.

After the event, use the saved screenshots and the contact details to reach out to the Super Achievers. Thank them for their time and for the value that they added, introduce yourself and, well you know the drill by now: Start the conversation by wanting to clarify something that they said or mentioned, Ask the 'Magic' question, find ways to add value to them and invest in building a relationship.

I have spoken at a few of these virtual events myself and so I can tell the story from the other side. As a speaker, you prepare in advance and make sure that you have your best material to offer to the audience. You show up on the day and you do your best to drop as much value as possible, but you don't always get the most response. You leave all your contact details and you try to make sure that people know how to get in touch.

Afterwards, you usually see a spike in the number of followers on social media and the number of subscribers, but usually, you do not get people personally reaching out and sending you a message. What I am trying to explain is that you will be one of the only people who send the speakers a message after the event. Most people are excited during the event and might even go and check out the speakers' profiles on social media, but very, very, very few people actually reach out and send a personal message.

Homework

Go online and find out about the relevant virtual summits, webinars and other online events happening in your field. The Facebook groups and online communities you have joined are a great way to find out about these events.

Action Deadline

"I am committed to...

_____

_____

_____

_____

_____

_____

_____

Therefore, by _____ I will have completed all my homework.

TurboCharged Takeaways

➤ The arrival of Coronavirus has led to an increase in the number of online and virtual events.

➤ Stay visible throughout the event and actively participate in all the discussions and activities.

➤ Don't overdo it and risk appearing as a spammer. Use thoughtful comments and thought-provoking questions to generate discussions.

➤ Use the Private Chat to build connections with other attendees. Enter them in a spreadsheet and prioritise them.

➤ Send everyone a message within 24 hours of the event, including the Super Achievers.

PART IV: TurboCharged Strategies

So far we have covered strategies that can be implemented immediately and will give you 'quick wins' to gain momentum in your networking journey. However, they have limitations due to their 'quick win' nature.

In this section of the book, I am going to cover strategies that are nothing short of a 'Silver Bullet' in the context of networking. But be aware that these strategies will take a lot of time, effort, energy and money to implement before you can use them to generate results. To use an analogy, the strategies that I have shared with you so far are like having the fastest car in the world to get around. The strategies that I will share with you now are like having a private jet! And just like a private jet, they take longer to acquire and require a lot more maintenance.

"Everybody has skills and talent, but not everybody has a strategy." Nitin Namdeo

Chapter Nine: Leveraging A Platform

"Relationships are the currency of business." Brian Basilico

Regardless of their field, business, background, industry, business, level of influence, or area of focus, what is the one thing that everyone wants more of?

Think about it…what is that thing that everybody, whom you want to connect with, is gunning for?

It's EXPOSURE!

Everyone wants more exposure. (Trust me, I know. This is exactly what I am looking for right now after writing this book) Therefore, if you build, or use an existing platform, you now have the keys to the door that they are hunting. You can offer them exposure as a primary means of adding value to them. We have already discussed the ways that you can add value to the Super Achievers, however, by having a platform as a means of adding value, you are placing yourself at the front of the herd and establishing yourself as a power player.

However, regardless of your platform choice, it takes a lot of time, effort, energy, patience and resilience to build a platform of your own from scratch or to leverage an existing platform. Both are viable options with huge potential for reward, however choosing between them depends on your goals, the amount of time you can dedicate and your personality.

Here is a list of common platforms that are available to you:

> Podcasts

Podcasts have taken off in recent years and they are a popular choice of platform to build your profile, attract the Super

Achievers and build a tribe of followers. There are podcasts on virtually every topic, from mindfulness to buying second-hand cars and everything in between. The two main types of podcasts are where the hosts bring on experts as guests and interview them or where the hosts hold a conversation, either between themselves or between them and the audience. Starting a podcast does take time, effort, money and patience, however, it can prove to be very rewarding, as not only do you get to use it as an incentive to attract the Super Achievers, but you can potentially build an audience and launch a business behind the podcast. The business can be centered around coaching, selling online products like courses/eBooks/merchandise or you can secure sponsorships from companies who want to expose your audience to their products and services. I am not a podcasting expert, so do your research, if you are interested, to find out more.

One of my friends from the States, Jon Belt, who is a high school English teacher, started a podcast (Teacher Tunnel podcast) to expose his fellow teachers to the teaching strategies of highly successful educators. He managed to get in front of all the people who he never would have met otherwise, simply because he was offering them exposure to his audience on his own platform that he independently built. His podcast was successful and he even started a business selling merchandise. He still maintained his job as a high school English Teacher and he still coached basketball after school, but with some determination, hard work and focus he managed to build a platform, attract an audience and even launched a business behind it. (Although, at the moment he is taking a break from the podcast and focusing on other ventures)

➢ Blogs

Blogging is huge! Just like podcasts, blogs are everywhere and they are about everything. You can write a blog yourself where you interview experts and leaders. Alternatively, you can ask them to make contributions to your blog too. There are lots of ways to monetise a blog. From selling your services, to affiliate marketing and running sponsored ads. It does take a long time to expand your blog and to build an audience, so lots of patience is needed.

➢ YouTube channel

There is more to YouTube than just watching cat videos all day. You can bring on guests and interview them for your audience. Video is the new currency of the world. You will have to learn a lot about video editing, the ever-changing YouTube algorithm, search engine optimisation, creating thumbnails and optimizing views, but it's a great platform that you can start building today. It will require some investment in technology etc. and it takes a lot of your time, but it's a solid choice if you are charismatic and confident in front of a camera. This was the platform of my choice as I prefer video to audio podcasts or blogs. I started my YouTube show as a hobby and when I first started, I literally didn't know anything about any of this stuff. I found out what I needed to know and then taught myself how to do it all. It was a long, slow and laborious process, but I am glad I did it. The results and the opportunities that come to me far outweighed the effort.

Despite the fact that I didn't end up with millions of subscribers and hordes of raving fans, I still managed to connect with and build relationships with some very influential people in the world. I interviewed them and then I actively looked for ways to add value to them and help them over time. This helped me develop my networking and relationship-building skills, hence, I am writing this book on networking instead of writing a book on achieving overnight success on YouTube.

> Social Media Accounts

There is also an option of starting an account and building an audience on a social platform of your choice. Make sure that it's where members of your potential audience hang around and that it is something that you are comfortable building. For example, don't start an Instagram account if you don't like taking and editing photos, or don't start a YouTube channel if you are camera shy and are searching for the Philosopher's Stone of charisma. It has to align with your skills, abilities and strengths. Then start generating high-level content and engage with the followers. You do need to have a deep knowledge of the subject you are talking about. If you are trying to 'fake it', you will be exposed and ripped to shreds on social in milliseconds. Once you have built it so that it's starting to gain momentum, you can use your social media presence to attract the Super Achievers.

Open the conversation with

"When was the last time you were featured on (enter the name of the platform where you have built your audience)?"

Take a few minutes and look at all the popular accounts on Instagram, Twitter, Facebook, SnapChat, TikTok, etc. You too can achieve what these people have created, just remember, there was a time when they too were in your shoes. A good starting point is to do some research by reading books, watching YouTube tutorials, doing online courses, reading articles and blogs, or even using the strategies in this book to network with Super Achievers of social media and learn directly from them.

Become a Contributor

You can write for an existing platform, instead of building your own platform from scratch. The advantages are obvious. You will already have an established platform with a following, credibility and all the 'behind-the-scenes' costs will be taken care of, such as marketing, web hosting, etc. You can write for a website, blog, magazine, newspaper, or you can film for a video platform like YouTube or Vimeo. You will have to work hard to produce output that is absolutely world-class in quality as there is a lot of competition for becoming a contributor, however, securing such a position will greatly boost your credibility and position.

When you approach a Super Achiever, just ask

"When was the last time you were featured on (enter the name of the platform you are contributing to)?" Game on!

Geoff Woods, former host of The Mentee podcast, went from being an employee to becoming an entrepreneur in just 10 months. Geoff became a contributing writer to Entrepreneur.com and also leveraged his own podcast to get in front of some of the most successful people in the world and opportunities exploded from everywhere. He became a partner with Gary Keller and Jay Papasan, the authors of *The One Thing*, and currently he is the Vice President of The ONE Thing and the host of The ONE Thing podcast, which is in the top 5% of all podcasts in the world. (You should totally 'Subscribe'. It's awesome!)

You can use the Homework exercise from chapter 3 and make a list of 5-10 people to call and share with them that you want to become a contributor to the platform of your choice.

Leverage your existing network to help you become a contributor to an existing platform.

Having shared all this, I would stress the fact that regardless of whether you decide to build your own platform from scratch or you decide to become a contributor to an existing platform, you will have to maintain consistency. It will require a lot of patience, time, effort, energy and even money to start something and build it to the point where it could be used as a tool. Even on an existing platform, you still need to work hard, consistently add value and build a name for yourself and a following.

However, doing so is more than worth it because the rewards far outweigh the investment. We cannot sit here, at this moment, and accurately predict the unique skills, experiences, and opportunities that you will gain by going through this process. The various stories of my friends, as well as my own story, confirm the uncertainty of success when we all started building and leveraging our platforms. However, none of us would be where we are if we hadn't started.

As a maths lecturer, when I started my YouTube channel, I could never have predicted that I would be able to connect with such high-profile people, or that I would be interviewed on multiple podcasts and radio shows, or that I would learn about and have the opportunities to make numerous investments, or that I would be featured in a book written by an International Bestselling author, or that I would end up writing a whole book on showing people how they can start building relationships with Super Achievers. These unforeseeable extraordinary consequences and more are possible for you too. The only limits will be the ones that you place on yourself.

"Without work, nothing prospers." Sophocles

The Plan

Hopefully, it is now clear to you that leveraging a platform is an extremely powerful strategy to help you connect with the Super Achievers, so now I am going to share with you my exact plan to put it into action.

➢   Create or Leverage a platform

Which platform you choose is completely up to you. You have lots of options. If you are an introvert, a blog will work for you. If you don't like being in front of a camera and creating videos, you can podcast instead. Creating your own platform will be more demanding, but you will have all the control. On the other hand, an existing platform can give you instant credibility, but it will not be your own. You will be adding value to someone else's platform and you will not have control over it. Whatever you decide, you will need to build your name, your reputation and a following to be successful.

➢   Update your social accounts with the details

Whatever social accounts you have, you need to keep them updated with the latest information about yourself and the projects that you are working on. Hence, when you have a platform sorted, you need to put that on your social accounts. This will help to raise awareness of what you are working on and it will also add substance to your online presence when someone looks you up.

➢   Produce high-level content consistently

Being persistently consistent is the key to creating extraordinary results. Plan in advance and invest time, energy and effort into creating high-level content that generates engagement. Engagement is the currency of social media. By engaging with the members of the audience you can identify what is working and what needs to be changed. The more you engage, the better your results will be.

I am not a social media expert so, I would highly recommend Gary Vaynerchuk's book *Jab, Jab, Jab, Right Hook* as it deals with developing high-quality content that's perfectly adapted to specific social media platforms and using the correct narrative particular to each different social platform.

➢ Share the content on your social

Once you have created and published the content, you then need to share it on all your social media to raise awareness and to show people what you are creating.

➢ Get business cards

It is definitely worth having the details of your platform and all your social media handles on a business card that you can share with people when you connect with them face-to-face. This business card doesn't have to have the details of your actual job, it can be exclusively for your platform and social accounts. Here is the business card that I used when I started my YouTube channel.

You can add the details of your social media accounts and contact details at the back of the card. Notice that the card only mentioned my YouTube channel, but didn't mention anything about my normal day job as a Maths Lecturer since it was not relevant. I used this card whenever I was asked by someone for my contact details whilst networking at events.

As I have mentioned earlier, it is perfectly fine to use business cards when connecting with people who are at the same level as you. Using the business cards in this way gives them instant access to the main places where they can learn more about you and your journey. On the other hand, it allows you to share with them all the places that you want them to visit and where they can go to follow you.

In summary, leveraging a platform is a strategy that I have used myself and it has also been employed by many others to expand their networks and TurboCharge their lives and businesses. My good friend Corey Poirier is an entrepreneur, International Bestselling author, multiple-time TEDx, MoMondays and PMx Speaker. He is also the host of the top-rated "Conversations with Passion" Radio Show and the founder of The Speaking Program. Corey, perhaps, used this strategy to its maximum effect as he has interviewed and connected with over 6500 of the world's top leaders, influencers and experts, such as Jack Canfield, Lisa Nichols, and Darren Hardy. Yup, that's a 65 with 2 zeros after it! How did he achieve all this? By leveraging his several podcasts, books and radio shows.

We all might not be able to achieve the heights that Corey has managed to achieve, but we can definitely follow in his footsteps. Remember, everyone is looking for more exposure and so by building or leveraging an existing platform you can fulfil this need.

You can combine both tactics and leverage an existing platform, while you build your own platform on the side. For example, you can become a contributor to a website or magazine while you start and build a podcast. Each piece of content you produce can be repurposed to suit both platforms. This will save you a lot of time and effort, as you won't have to produce different content for each platform, however, you will gain some serious influence by having multiple platforms and offering maximum exposure to the Super Achievers with only a minimum investment of their time.

"Every next level of your life will demand a different you."
Leonardo DiCaprio

Leveraging a platform allows you to bring massive credibility to each interaction because you are demonstrating that you are an 'Active Agent' in the field/industry. It moves your position from being a 'Passive Consumer' of content to an 'Active Producer' of content. It also allows you to build social proof that people can verify by viewing and engaging with your content. Over time all your content and social proof become a digital online portfolio of all your work which will boost your credibility and influence to soaring heights that you can leverage to create new unique life-changing opportunities and gain access to ultra-high-level Super Achievers and their networks.

Lastly, your content and social proof will 'work for you' even when you are sleeping or are busy with your daily life. Your digital online portfolio will always exist in cyberspace and it will continue to attract attention for you, but it will also make an impact in the lives of others who need to hear your story and get your perspective in order to work through their problems and achieve their goals. By producing content, you have the potential to make a big impact and change lives, not only during your lifetime, but also after you have departed from this world.

Personally, I believe that it is our duty to leave behind a strong legacy that will continue to make an impact, even after we are gone and creating content by leveraging a platform allows us to do just that.

TurboCharged Takeaways

➢ Everyone wants more exposure, so leveraging a platform allows you to fulfil this fundamental, yet high-priority need of all the Super Achievers.

➢ Building your own platform and your own audience is extremely powerful and comes with a high level of credibility that you can leverage to your advantage. However, it requires time and patience to grow it before it can be used as a tool.

➢ Leveraging a platform can fast-track your networking journey, however, you will not own the platform or the content and so you will not have any control over them.

➢ You can leverage an existing platform, whilst you build yours on the side for maximum effect. However, that requires some serious commitment.

➢ The rewards far outweigh the investment, so decide on your course of action and start executing.

In the next chapter, you will learn the 'Unorthodox Approach' that has the potential to give you better results.

Chapter Ten: The Unorthodox Approach

"The greatest act of love is to pay attention." Dawn Sawyer

Who are the people that parents love the most? Good guess, but no. Babysitters is not the correct answer here. Parents love people who are kind, caring, loving and attentive to their children. So, the quickest and easiest way to get someone to like you is to be nice to their kids. Projecting this in a broader context, we naturally like people who are caring and attentive to the people we care about. If a stranger is nice to us, we think that they are a good person. On the other hand, if a stranger is kind and attentive to our family and friends, the people we love and care about, they fast-track themselves to our gratitude, respect and trust zone.

Fun fact: Super Achievers are not immune to this.

To wormhole your way into the hearts of the Super Achievers (some technical jargon that I have just invented) that you want to connect with, you need to find out who are the most important people in the lives of these Super Achievers. Mostly, the Super Achievers are hounded by everyone from all directions, like a proverbial flame surrounded by metaphorical moths, but no one pays attention to the people around them because they feel that it's a waste of time. The family and friends of the Super Achievers get ignored all the time and, here's the most important thing to remember, they notice! They notice that they are being ignored and that no one is paying any attention to them. A lot of the time, people don't even recognise their presence. How would you feel if your existence wasn't even recognised?

Your job is simple, once you know who the most important people are in the life of the Super Achiever you are trying to connect with, use what you have learnt so far in this book to start building a relationship with them. Be authentically curious and show genuine interest in what they are working on, what are their challenges and where do they need help. Find a way to solve their problems and help them with their work. Add value to them and start a friendship.

Sending them a present also works wonders because they almost never receive anything as people keep buying presents for just the Super Achiever. Discover their hobbies, interests and the causes they care about and just buy them a gift or make a donation to their favourite cause, with no strings attached and without any expectations. Do it because you genuinely want to be friends with them. Actions speak louder than words, so prove your intentions.

On the surface, this may seem like the long way round to connect with the Super Achiever, since you are spending all this time, effort and energy connecting with the person who is not actually your target. However, in many cases, it is actually the shortcut that everyone ignores precisely because of this mindset. A lot of the time, the Super Achievers actively put obstacles in front of themselves in order to make it difficult for people to have access to them. If they didn't put these obstacles, then they would never get a minute's peace and they actually wouldn't have a life at all. Therefore, not only do you have to compete with everyone else for the Super Achiever's attention, but you also have to overcome these invisible obstacles. Would you rather take your chances swimming against the current or are you willing to change your route to get to your destination quicker, with much less effort?

Of course, there will be times when this is not going to be the most effective strategy and that is fine. The main aim of using this strategy is to get a personal recommendation from the person who is closest to the Super Achiever. Just imagine you getting a personal recommendation where Mark Zuckerburg's (Billionaire founder of Facebook) wife is speaking high praises of you and tells Mark that he definitely needs to connect with you because you are amazing and you have really helped her out. (This is an extreme example, but you get the idea.)

To put it simply, the Super Achievers are in the spotlight all the time, but the person who is special to them is not under the same level of spotlight, so it's much easier to gain access to that person.

Below is the list of the people who the Super Achievers might care about:

➤ Spouse/Partner
➤ Kids
➤ Parents
➤ Assistant
➤ Employees
➤ Pets
➤ Friends
➤ Business partners
➤ Coaches/Mentors/Trainers
➤ Mentees

This list is not exhaustive and is not in any particular order. Look out for anyone from the above list when you are searching social media for your research. If you see them being mentioned in posts, pictures, interviews, videos, tags, etc. then that is a strong indication that they are someone who the Super Achiever loves and cares about.

A little while after I started my YouTube channel, I connected with a very high-level Super Achiever (I am protecting their name on purpose). It was completely baffling to me at the time that someone like that would even consider talking to me. They were an international power player and I was a humble maths lecturer who started a YouTube channel without even knowing how to edit a 5-second video clip. I couldn't believe it! By following them on Instagram I discovered that they have 2 cats who they love and care for very much. They posted pictures of their cats all the time. The crazy thing was, I love cats too. (I have 2 right now. I know, what was I thinking, right? But the cuteness is tooooooooooo much to handle!)

Anyways, I managed to get the interview done for my YouTube channel, but I didn't just want to be another interviewer since that Super Achiever gets hundreds of interviews every year. I wanted to go further and build a relationship. So, I bought laser toys for the cats, wrapped them very carefully and beautifully, wrote a handwritten note on coloured sugar paper and sent that as a present for the cats. How do you think it went?

My present was received extremely well and I received a very grateful email with pictures of the cats. I know that we shared a mutual love for cats, so I didn't just stop there. I sent pictures of my cat (at the time I only had one) and I also bought funny and interesting books about cats and sent them to the Super Achiever over time. This started a friendship and built a relationship around our common love for cats. However, it was a genuine gesture. I wasn't faking it. I put a lot of thought, effort, time and money into those presents.

Having said all this, I do need to clarify that once you have managed to connect with the Super Achiever, given that you have played your cards right and everything works out, you do NOT then stop the relationship with the person you connected with. They are the reason that you managed to get in front of the Super Achiever. They were not a means to an end. The entire focus of this book is on showing you how you can build relationships and once you have built a relationship, the focus should then be on strengthening it. They should not feel any difference in their relationship with you afterwards, otherwise, they are going to see you as a manipulative (insert appropriate insult). Do not ignore them! Their relationship with you is unique and should be treated and nurtured as such.

This also holds true even if your relationship with the Super Achiever does not go according to plan or if the Super Achiever is not able to support you with your goals and problems. Maintain the relationship. Support them and keep adding value to them. Who knows, maybe another opportunity might present itself later. Do not 'fake it' at any point. They will see right through it (remember that study about intuition?). No amount of money can buy you a close intimate relationship with a Super Achiever, but you can build it yourself with time, effort and patience.

Connecting and building a relationship with a Super Achiever also does not give you the right to then show off about your 'achievement'. It just makes you look cheap, cocky and a complete moron. You must also never share any personal or contact details of the Super Achiever or their loved ones with others. It's a matter you trust! You need to protect their privacy and savagely guard your relationship with them. You need to establish integrity and build a reputation for yourself so that the Super Achievers are happy to stay in contact with you and are also willing to introduce you to the people in their network.

This can be extremely powerful as just one Super Achiever introducing you to their network of ultra-high-level individuals can collapse weeks, months, or years of time. You are leveraging your current network to expand your Sphere of Influence, instead of going back to ground zero and then starting the whole process from scratch to connect with someone new. By now, if you have added enough value to the Super Achiever and you have been genuine, authentic, polite and respectful then they would be happy to introduce you to others in their circle.

Leveraging your 'Super' Network

Essentially, this can be another strategy with its own chapter because it's such a powerful tool. After adding enough value to a Super Achiever and building trust, they would probably ask you what they can do to help you and at that point, you can share the profile of the type of people you are trying to connect with and ask them to make an introduction with someone who might be a good fit. Bingo! You do not need to connect with 30 or 300 or 3000 or 30,000 Super Achievers to achieve extraordinary results. You just need to connect with 3 and then, after you have added massive value to them and the time is right, you can ask to be introduced to others in their network. (Maybe you already have someone specific in mind).

You repeat the patterns and add massive value to your new contacts and then ask to be introduced to the people in their network and so on. This means that you will have a few high-quality deep relationships with a handful of Super Achievers, instead of having hundreds of people in your network, most of whom you will know only as well as the smell of roses from Mars.

This is exactly how I expanded my network and secured so many high-level interviews on my YouTube show. I made sure that the person I was interviewing had an amazing experience, I added as much value to them as I could and at the end, I just asked them if they could refer someone else who would be a good fit for my show. This meant that I didn't have to start each new relationship from scratch. Instead, someone from their Sphere of Influence made the introduction and so they were happy to connect with me and arrange an interview. Essentially, each new contact was a 'warm lead' because they already knew about me.

The fact is that once you connect with someone you, potentially, then have access to their whole network. Would that require you to show up as your best self and be genuinely curious, authentic, add value first, have patience and build trust? Absolutely! Would your life accelerate at the speed of light when you finally achieve this? Heck yea!

The 8th 'Golden Rule'

Knowing what you know now, it's time to introduce another 'Golden Rule'.

> ➤ No existing relationship should suffer as a result of new ones.

I can't stress this enough! You can use these strategies and build a solid network and surround yourself with Super Achievers, but if you are in it for the glory or you are just chasing the 'next-best-thing', you are really missing the point. The real value is in building, cultivating and nurturing these relationships.

"Saying hello doesn't have any ROI. It's about building relationships." Gary Vaynerchuk

Don't lose touch with the people whom you connected with at the start and don't ignore someone just because you now know someone who is further ahead than they are. Treat everyone with the same level of respect whether they are a Super Achiever, someone a Super Achiever cares about, or someone that a Super Achiever connected you with.

TurboCharged Takeaways

➢ Everyone hounds the Super Achievers for their attention from all directions every day, so they are always in the spotlight.

➢ The people Super Achievers care about are not in the same spotlight. Use social media to find out who they are and connect with them.

➢ Find out what they are working on and where they need help and then add value to them. You want to help them so they can't help but recommend you to the Super Achiever in their life.

➢ Nurture all the existing relationships as you cultivate new ones. Do not let existing relationships suffer because of new ones.

In the next chapter, I will share with you the strategy with a nearly 100% success rate.

Chapter 11: The Strategy with Almost 100% Success Rate

"The richest people in the world look for and build networks, everyone else looks for work." Robert Kiyosaki

Yeah. I know! That's a very bold title, but this is the one strategy that has nearly always borne me fruit. So, here we go…

When is the one time when Super Achievers are actively searching to meet as many people as they can? Nope! It's not when they don't have change for the coffee machine. The only time when Super Achievers are actively searching to meet people is when they are looking to promote something that they are launching. It might be a new book, podcast, online course, website, award, business, partnership, talk, etc. This is the one time when they want to be in front of as many people as possible. They want all eyes on them and the number of eyeballs really matters!

Sometimes, the path to cultivating a relationship with a Super Achiever is not that simple. It might even look damn near impossible after you have tried almost everything else. However, if you keep searching social media for clues on whether they are talking about a particular product, service, or achievement that they are working on, then that is when the Super Achiever is going to look for exposure to promote it. At that time, they would be happy to talk to anyone who can help them promote themselves and their newest accomplishment. This would be the perfect time for you to reach out and offer your help.

Remember Chapter 8 where we talked about leveraging a platform as a way to immediately add value to the Super Achievers by giving them exposure? Yup! You are right. This is the time when having a platform really makes a difference. I have found this to be extremely effective and it has allowed me to connect with several 'unreachables' and Super Achievers including:

➢ Dorie Clark – Full profile on page 152

➢ Gene McNaughton – Full profile on page 155

➢ Corey Poirier – Full profile on page 164

The timing here is critical. I reached out to them when they had all launched a new book. Earlier, I told you that it took me 2 years to get in front of Gene McNaughton, however, I waited patiently until he had launched his new book *The Sales E.D.G.E* and that is when I finally managed to get an appointment and do an interview with Gene. It can be a waiting game, however, if you are clear on who you want to connect with and if you are patient, you can eventually find a way to get in front of whomever you want.

The story is very similar with Dorey Clark and Corey Poirier as they both also had their new books published. Dorey had launched *Entrepreneurial You* and Corey was launching *The Book of Why*. However, because I was following them on social media and listening to their appearances on podcasts, I was aware of the book launches and so I grabbed the opportunity as soon as I got the chance. I reached out to them specifically referencing the different podcasts they had appeared on, the interview specifics, I congratulated them on their new books, and then offered them the opportunity for an interview on my YouTube show. BOOM! Money in the bank!

This strategy works best with a newly launched product or service, however, there is no reason why you can't use an existing product or service and use that as a leverage point to reach out to the Super Achievers. The main reason that it works best with new launches is that the Super Achievers themselves are actively trying to look for opportunities to promote their products or services. With existing products and services, they have already gone through the 'active' promotional phase and are probably now in the 'passive' promotional phase, relying on marketing and recommendations to promote them. That doesn't mean that you shouldn't try though.

Having said that, the reason why I am sharing this with you is to show you how this strategy worked for me and get you excited about the possibilities that you might be able to create for yourself. Like everything else that I have shared with you in this book, if you feel that there is a better way to do it then I want you to do it that way instead. I am sharing with you what has worked for me; however, I fully recognise that my way is not the only way.

Also, if you do not have a platform or you do not want to invest time and build a platform of your own, then I suggest that you use the strategies we have discussed so far and build relationships with authors, podcast hosts, radio hosts and other media influencers with an audience. This is so that you can reach out to the Super Achiever when they launch their product and offer to make an introduction with the appropriate media influencer where they can go and promote it.

It would be useful to check with the media influencer first to see if they are willing to connect and interview the Super Achiever before making the introduction. Doing so would again position you as a person of value, but this is not as powerful as having your own platform. It will still allow you to connect with them and you can start the conversation and work on building a relationship, however, having your own platform that you have worked to grow adds more credibility.

Ideally, you want to have a platform and also have connections with other media influencers. That way, once you have added value by interviewing them on your platform, you can continue to add value by giving them more exposure via other media influencers and their audiences. It shows the strength of your network and the high level of value that you can deliver.

The Power of ROI

Look at it from the perspective of the Super Achievers, they get a lot of exposure and value just by connecting with one person-you. And all without putting in any extra effort to promote their new product or service. For them the 'Return On Investment' is huge! They only have to know you and spend time with you to gain access to so many new contacts and opportunities that they wouldn't have to actively look for and develop themselves.

This idea of ROI is the biggest mindset shift that I share whenever someone asks me how they can build and grow relationships with Super Achievers. This is extremely powerful, especially if you continue to consistently provide the Super Achievers with contacts and opportunities over time. In essence, you don't want to leave a single shred of doubt in their mind that you are someone who belongs in their network. Furthermore, you are also making deposits in their 'Reciprocity Impulse'. After all the value you have added to them, they will be aching to pay you back when the time comes.

When making introductions and referrals, it is important to ensure that the connection is a good fit and both parties will benefit from the interaction. This is your responsibility towards your network because they are trusting you. You need to build trust, maintain your integrity and protect your reputation. Don't fall for the short-term gains, as some people might offer you opportunities or money for a connection with a Super Achiever. Always protect and be loyal to your network. There is no exception to this eternal law!

"Your network is your net worth." Tim Sanders

In summary, if ever in doubt about making an introduction, don't do it.

"Better to be safe, than sorry." Samuel Lover

Leveraging *Reviews* for Attention

Another powerful way to add value to a Super Achiever and to attract their attention is to leave an amazing review for their product or service. Obviously, this requires you to have used the product or service yourself before you leave the review. In my experience, this strategy works best with books because sometimes their courses, online programs, coaching packages, etc. are very expensive. If you can afford to purchase them, then that's fantastic. Otherwise, reading their book(s) and writing a review totally works.

All you have to do is to buy the book, read it and leave a stunning review. Most of the time the reviews that people leave are short and vague. However, if you leave an honest detailed review explaining how specifically you are using the different strategies, tactics and ideas, you are definitely going to catch their attention. Write the review and then send them a message and tell them that you have read their book and you have left a review and now you want to connect. You can offer to interview them and feature them on your platform. This will massively improve the chances of them replying and connecting with you because you have added value to them even before sending the initial message. When they check they will see that you have put a lot of time, effort and thought into your review and they are very likely to reply to your message even if it is just to say 'Thank You'.

I am sharing with you an example of one of the book reviews that I wrote to get you started. Simply visit the link at the start of the book on "Before You Read" - page viii to download the pdf file.

(P.S. Don't forget to leave a stunning 5-star review for this book on Amazon.)

TurboCharged Takeaways

➤ Super Achievers are looking for exposure when they launch a new product or service, so keep an eye on their social and reach out to them when the time is right.

➤ Make a connection and offer to interview them for your platform. If you don't have your own platform, introduce them to the media influencers in your network.

➤ Ideally, interview them on your platform and then refer them to other media influencers in your network to add maximum value.

➤ Don't for the short-term gains. Protect your network and guard your reputation. Always be loyal to your network.

➤ Better safe than sorry.

➤ Read their book and leave a detailed, honest, thoughtful review. Then contact them and offer to interview them on your platform.

In the next chapter, we will talk about how to stay in touch with your network regularly and fix a time slot in your calendar to make sure that it gets done.

Chapter Twelve: Staying in Touch

"One of the greatest gifts you can give to anyone is the gift of your attention." Jim Rohn

Whilst you need to allocate a certain level of focus on growing your network and connecting and bringing more amazing people into your life, you also want to ensure that you can maintain what you have already built. You want to periodically contact and stay in touch with everyone you have connected with so far and continue to add value to them. You don't want to fall off their radar.

You have spent a lot of time, effort and energy into building your network and so you don't want it to slip through your fingers now that you have finally made it. Don't rely on others to stay in touch. Everyone has a busy life and everyone has commitments that demand their constant attention and focus.

Therefore, make it your responsibility to stay in contact with everyone. Even the people whom you connected with at the start of your journey. They might not be at the ultra-high level like the people later in your journey, but you must not forget about them. Remember, they are the ones who helped you get started.

Having said this, you will also get busier as you progress in your journey. The demands of life and business will pile up and you will have to adapt and rise to the challenge. Therefore, you need a system to help you stay on track. Setting up a simple spreadsheet with everyone's details, the last date when you contacted them and a space to record comments about the last interaction can be a very useful tool to have. Of course, there are many advanced platforms and paid CRM systems to help you with all this and you can absolutely get them if you want.

However, I believe that if you can get an 85% solution that is easy to set up with a simple spreadsheet and doesn't cost you anything, then it will be sufficient. With a little effort and planning, you can track your contacts and stay in touch with them. Unless you have a career or business that revolves around networking and you indeed need a professional CRM system with all the advanced features, in which case it actually makes sense to make the investment.

Again, leverage the power of your phone's calendar and put a weekly time block of at least 30 mins, or whatever you feel is an appropriate period of time, solely for the purpose of getting in touch with everyone in your network. (Do it now because 'later' never happens!) You can also put the time slot in your diary or planner; however, I prefer the phone calendar as it's something that you probably carry with you all the time. Also, it reminds you automatically when the time comes, so you can put it in the calendar and forget about it and carry on with your daily routines.

Obviously, you will have to prioritise staying in touch with certain people more, compared to others. Remember how we categorized our contacts according to priority in Chapter 8? You can use the same system here. Personally, for high-priority contacts, I would recommend getting in touch at least once every few weeks. That way you can stay up-to-date with what's happening in their life. Any longer and you risk drifting too far apart and then it can be challenging to build that closeness again. Just be aware that, inevitably, you will lose touch with some people over time. Be OK with that.

132

Furthermore, you will also stay 'current' in everyone else's mind. This will maximise your chances of attracting new relationships and opportunities. If you are in the back of everyone's mind while they go about their normal routines, it is very likely that they will reach out to you when they come across something that will add value to you. This is why it's so important to come from a place of service and add value to them first so that they are willing to reciprocate and add value back to you.

On the other hand, if you are not on the grid, then it is very likely that you will be in the back of everyone's mind and, as a result, you are not going to attract as many relationships and opportunities.

Providing LTV

One of the questions that I get asked often is how to maintain relationships with people in your network over time. I believe that the most important element to consider is the Long Term Value (LTV) that you can provide. Essentially, LTV means that you continuously find new ways to add value to the people in your network over a long period of time. Typically, over a long enough timeline, all relationships and friendships fizzle out unless intentionally and continuously reignited. I have found that the easiest way to continuously provide Long Term Value to my network is by acting as a SuperConnector.

As my network expands and I meet more amazing and interesting people, I make introductions between them and the people in my current network. As I mentioned in the last chapter, before making any introductions I always make sure that there is alignment and that it will prove to be mutually beneficial for everyone.

Providing LTV to people in your network gives them a disproportionate ROI for connecting with you. They are continuously going to get value from you and therefore, they would want to stay in touch and maintain the relationship with you over a long period of time. This is especially true when you are acting as a SuperConnector because everyone in your network will get access to new contacts and opportunities outside of their Sphere of Influence, which they would not have access to otherwise.

Making Spellbinding Introductions

When I am making an introduction, I never make an introduction like this:

"Hi

Jen, meet Jack.

Jack, meet Jen.

I hope you guys have fun connecting.

Tallal"

This is completely useless for both Jack and Jen since they do not know anything about each other and I didn't give them anything to talk about. I also didn't tell them why I think it would be good for them to connect with each other. Instead, my introductions look like this:

"Hi both

I wanted to make this intro because I believe that there is great alignment here.

134

Dorie, meet Janice. Janice and I connected recently via a mutual contact, we jumped on a call and became friends quickly. Janice is a LinkedIn expert and during our call, Janice gave me some brilliant advice which led me to change my profile picture on LinkedIn. Janice is also the host of The Relationships Rule podcast and she is a Master Networker. Janice is very open and giving and I absolutely love talking to her. She has a special way of making you feel warm and welcome with her presence.

Janice, meet my very close friend Dorie. Dorie is the #1 Ranked Communication Coach, Top 50 Business Thinkers in the world, she also consults and speaks for Google, Microsoft, and The World Bank. Dorie's new book 'THE LONG GAME' is due to be released later this year and currently, Dorie is looking to talk about her book by serving others. The most unforgettable thing about Dorie is her magnetic ability to attract everyone with her ever-present radiant smile. I believe that Dorie would be a perfect guest for your podcast.

I now leave this with you both

Appreciate you 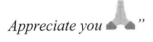 *"*

I adapted this approach from Vanessa Van Edward, who talks about being a *"Raver"* and a *"Highlighter"* when making introductions in her book *"Captivate"*. Notice how my introduction is extremely thorough and how I absolutely "raved" about each of the people above whilst introducing them to the other. I also "highlighted" something that I think makes them special. For Janice, it was her "warm...presence". For Dorie, it was her "ever-present radiant smile". It shows that I really care, that I have been really paying attention to the person and I know what makes them special.

I also, introduced them in such a way that they know what they can talk about and why I think this introduction was important. Dorie is launching her new book and is a top thought leader in the business world. Janice has a podcast and she serves business owners via her expertise and her podcast and is looking for top experts to interview.

It also shows the level of thought, care, and effort I put into making the introduction, which, in turn, demonstrates the level of respect and care that I have for people in my network. I believe that if I make a weak introduction, then it will lead to a weak connection between the people I have introduced. I hope that sharing this example will help you when you are making your introductions. I really want to thank both Dorie Clark and Janice Porter for allowing me to include this here to share with you.

Focus on the Present

When you are connecting with your network, always focus on how you can help them RIGHT NOW. Your focus should not be on what happened in the past, but on where they are at now and what is currently happening in their lives and businesses. A lot of the time their current situation is not obvious, therefore, you might have to do some digging. The best way to elicit this information is to focus on powerful questions during the conversation, such as the ones below:

➢ What are they working on right now? / What are they focused on right now? / What projects are they dealing with right now?

➢ What are the new challenges that they are facing? / What are they struggling with right now?

➤ What are their new achievements? / What are they celebrating right now? / What are they most excited about right now?

➤ Did they manage to overcome previous challenges? / Did they break through the past problems and limitations?

I would highly recommend reading Dorie Clark's LinkedIn Newsletter post titled: "How to become Dramatically Effective at Networking", where Dorie shares the follow-up strategies for staying in touch with your contacts.[6]

---

[6]https://www.linkedin.com/pulse/welcome-dorie-clark-linkedin-newsletter-dorie-clark/

TurboCharged Takeaways

➤   Periodically contact and stay in touch with everyone you have connected with so far and continue to add value to them.

➤   Put a weekly time block in your phone calendar to connect with everyone in your network.

➤   Set up a simple spreadsheet with everyone's details and the last date when you contacted them.

➤   Get in touch at least once a month, so you can stay up-to-date with what's happening in their life. This will also keep you 'current' in everyone's mind.

➤   Read Dorie Clark's LinkedIn newsletter post titled "How to become Dramatically Effective at Networking" and her book titled "Stand Out Networking".

Final Words

"I cannot do all the good that the world needs. But the world needs all the good that I can do." Jana Stanfield.

Did you know that research shows that helping and serving others is directly related to higher levels of happiness? This is part of the reason why there is a great focus on adding value, helping others and coming from a place of service in this book. Social psychologist, Elizabeth Dunn, found this link through her groundbreaking work on what makes us happy. Beyond research, she found this to be true in her own life as she personally experienced this link between helping others and higher levels of happiness, which validated her research. She tells this incredible story in her TED talk[7].

Networking is typically seen as a subject that only belongs in the corporate and business worlds and is mainly associated with sales, numbers, transactions, money, and falling victim to sly tactics that force you to make a decision.

However, that is a very narrow way of looking at networking. By networking and adding value to others, not only are we setting up our domino run to success, but we also gain spiritual benefits of gaining more happiness and fulfilment. This is because there is an actual biological reward that we receive when we are of service to others. Dopamine and other 'happiness hormones' are released in our brains when we actively and intentionally engage in developing Human Connection.

---

[7] https://www.youtube.com/watch?v=lUKhMUZnLuw

Networking = Human Connection

I believe that life is a people business, where instead of transactions we have interactions and the currency of exchange is mutual respect, kind words, and a smile. I also believe that networking is where we intentionally and purposefully develop and deepen Human Connection.

This means that we are networking every time we interact with someone, regardless of whether they are a business titan or our grandparents. And so, the core principles of polite, pleasant, positive, respectful human interaction also apply to the business world and the 'networking strategies' to connect and build relationships with the Super Achievers also apply to everyday life. We are all humans and our common shared values of mutual respect, compassion, love, empathy, care and kindness are the key ingredients to living a happy and fulfilled life.

What I am trying to say is that we cannot limit networking to just business interactions because it is a part of every interaction. Helping others, adding value and coming from a place of service are part of a fundamental mindset that we need to cultivate. The 'culture' of networking will inevitably become toxic if we continue to only view it through a narrow lens and apply it only to the business world because then it just becomes a 'medium of transaction'.

I believe that networking is just another name for purposeful and intentional Human Connection. I also believe that it is the universal law guiding every positive successful human interaction and that by cultivating this wider mindset and applying it to every interaction we have, not only can we TurboCharge our lives and our businesses, but it is essential in collaborating together and finding new creative solutions to the big wicked problems of our world.

The equation is simple: *Care + Value + Service = Human Connection,* but it must be purposeful and intentional. The difference between a random interaction vs networking is that networking is not random, it's purposeful and intentional.

Too often our interactions are 'random' and without clarity on how the interaction will result in an increase in Relationship Capital, or we are focused on achieving the 'agenda' behind the conversation /appearance, be it, "I want to be liked." "I want to look good." "I want to be seen as a pro." "I want to get (insert random thought)." I believe that we need to set the intention to follow the 'Golden Rules', connect deeply and build strong relationships with our interactions.

We must focus on the person behind the words of the conversation. Every one of us is made of hopes, dreams, ambitions, wants, hurts, pain, creativity, love, passion, empathy, compassion, kindness, respect and so much more. I believe that this is the person, behind the conversation/appearance, that we need to reach out to and connect with.

So, don't underestimate the power of a smile, a random act of kindness, or a spontaneous urge to help someone in need because in those moments you are powerfully connecting with other people and potentially building deep relationships. As a result, you are building a world-class network. Below I will show you 2 examples from my private conversations with people to illustrate this and to emphasise the importance of Human Connection

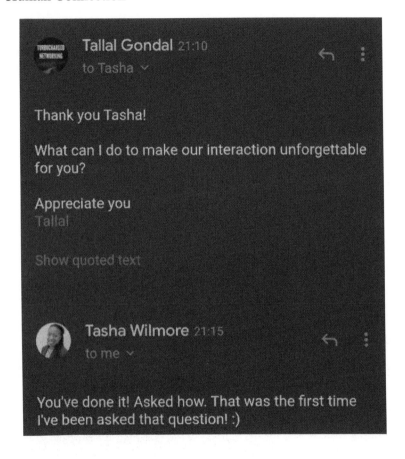

Thank you Tasha!

What can I do to make our interaction unforgettable for you?

Appreciate you
Tallal

Show quoted text

Tasha Wilmore 21:15
to me

You've done it! Asked how. That was the first time I've been asked that question! :)

A close friend introduced me to one of his contacts and Tasha, her Executive Assistant, helped me to book a call with her. I am sure that Tasha meets and interacts with a lot of people and helps them book calls, as she did for me. However, I wanted to go beyond the typical interaction and build a real connection with Tasha, so I sent her the above message from a place of Care, Value, and Service. I had already got what I wanted and I could have stopped there, but I focused on the human behind the conversation, I focused on Tasha and genuinely tried to make an effort to connect with her and make her feel special. You can see Tasha's reaction for yourself. Later, I asked Tasha if I could include it here in the book as an example to share with you and she happily agreed.

> Hi ███████ Hope you are safe, well and crushing it. How can I support you right now?
>
> ♥ 1

23 May 2021, 22:38

> Event that question is pretty freakin magical - thank you Tallal 🙏
> I actually can't tell you the last time I was asked that

Here is another example from a conversation with a friend, who is a successful Holistic Therapist and entrepreneur from New Zealand. She asked me to keep her name anonymous and therefore, I have respected her wishes. Observe the 'Love Heart' reaction to my message and her response.

In both these cases, I did not require any knowledge of the latest logarithms, technological trends, newest platforms, or the 38.261 steps to (fill in the blank). All I had to do was ask a simple question that demonstrated to the other person that I

143

cared about them and made them feel special. This is because mostly, people do not remember us for what we said to them, but rather how we made them feel. I believe that by fully taking control of the feeling we leave others with, we can TurboCharge our interactions to build deep, authentic, and meaningful long-term relationships.

The 'Accelerators' of Life

Moreover, I believe that there are certain 'Accelerators' that can help us boost our growth and our results. Some people call them 'Multipliers' or 'Catalysts', however, they are all the same. The 'Accelerators' can give us a clear advantage and help us achieve results faster. They are:

Knowledge – by having more knowledge or having access to new creative ideas we can gain a clear advantage and achieve results faster.

Technology – possessing the most advanced, most powerful and most effective technologies we can achieve more, in less time, with low costs and overheads.

Resources – from land, raw materials, and water to new innovative products, targeted platforms and powerful systems. By having more resources and having access to specialized systems we can fast-track our path to success.

Opportunities – everyone knows the value of the perfect opportunity because it can launch you into the stratosphere of success. Without it, things may never change.

Money – don't need to explain this one, I think.
144

With this in the backdrop, I want to present to you the idea that the 'Master Key' to unlock and unleash all these Accelerators is People. It is people who discover and have Knowledge. It is people who develop and use technology. It is people who create, manipulate, own, and process Resources. It is people who are the 'gatekeepers' of opportunities. It is people who earn, spend, and have Money. Therefore, building relationships with people is the most important and the most powerful 'Accelerator' of them all! It is unfortunate indeed just how often we lose sight of this fact.

Care. Value. Service. These are the 3 words that are the essence of TurboCharged Networking. Without them, we cannot develop the Human Connection, build relationships and unlock the 'Master Key' to the Accelerators of Life.

Paying it Forward

The final piece of advice that I will share with you is to pay it forward. You might not be a Super Achiever yet or maybe you are, but you can always turn around and help someone who is a few steps behind you. Share what you have learned from this book and through your experiences. Help them see the possibilities that they can create for themselves and believe in their potential. They will really appreciate the help, just like you would really appreciate receiving help and support from someone who is further ahead than you. Remember, maybe not too long ago you were exactly where they are now.

"Don't just look for your miracle. Become someone else's miracle." Joel Osteen

No one succeeds alone. This is one of the main reasons why a lot of Super Achievers want to help others who are just starting out. They remember that there were others who helped them when they were starting out and how crucial that help was in allowing them to get where they are today. After you have started on your journey, it is important that you not only help and add value to the Super Achievers that you are connecting with, but also help others who are behind you. They might not even have the clarity on how to get started, but you can share your experience with them and help them in gaining that clarity.

Just as someone out there might have the solution to all your problems and the roadmap to all your goals, you might have the solution to someone else's problems and the roadmap to their goals.

I believe that Zig Zigler's famous quote best encapsulates the main message behind this book, *"You can have everything in life you want if you will just help enough other people get what they want."*

Conclusion

At the start of the book, I presented you with a simple idea that we are the average of the 5 people we spend the most time with and I presented the case that by upgrading those 5 people we can get solutions to all our problems, get the roadmap to achieve all our goals and create extraordinary opportunities for ourselves and our businesses.

The rest of the book focused on introducing the concepts that will help you to cultivate the mindset of a world-class networker and the practical strategies that will allow you to find, connect and build relationships with anyone, whether they are a Super Achiever or not. I shared with you practical tips on how to overcome Social Anxiety and how to Maintain the Connection. I also took you behind-the-scenes and shared with you stories, messages, and examples of what my journey looked like and what worked for me at those times. I hope that what I have shared actually serves you.

Everything I have mentioned is based on my own experience and I fully realise that there are other ideas, strategies, and approaches to networking. However, I am proud to say that what I have shared with you is the best of what I know and what has worked for me. I urge you to take action on what you have learned from this book, but if you find something that complements or enhances anything that I have mentioned here, then adapt your strategy and use it alongside what I have shared in this book.

The mention of any other networking strategies, tactics, and advice are beyond the scope of his book. Who knows, maybe one day I might write another book.

As I said earlier, no one succeeds alone. I started my networking journey in 2016 after I listened to Geoff Woods on season 1 of the Mentee podcast utter the Jim Rohn quote, "You are the average of the 5 people you spend the most time with." Since then, I have been fascinated by the idea of surrounding myself with powerful people and learning from them. Whatever I learned from Geoff and others, I always put it to practice.

An extremely important lesson that I have learned along the way is that the true power of networking does not lie in connecting and building relationships with everyone, but rather it lies in intentionally connecting and purposefully surrounding ourselves with the right people to build our own 'Tribe'. This will drastically increase our chances of living a more fulfilled, enjoyable, and successful life. Especially, when it's a 'Tribe' that consists of people who are at or above our level of skills, competence, experience, and knowledge. Through their continuous guidance, mentoring, advice, and support, we can avoid all the mistakes, gain several lifetimes of wisdom and knowledge and collapse our timeline to success.

Along my journey, I have fallen and failed more times than I have succeeded, but I would gladly do it all over again if I had to. My final advice to you is:

Make sure to celebrate all your victories along with your networking, business, and life's journey, especially the small ones. We need to celebrate the small victories so we can call on them and use them to fuel us in times of need to push past adversity, defy the odds, and achieve extraordinary results.

Don't be phased by failures. There will probably be quite a few. Failures are a part of life. It's best that we acknowledge them and understand their value in helping us to reflect on how we can improve ourselves and what we could have done

148

differently. View each failure as a chance to learn, improve and accelerate by coming back better, stronger, and wiser than before. When you fail, it's time to evaluate, pivot, rise up and continue fighting.

"Victory is always possible for the person who refuses to stop fighting." Napoleon Hill

TurboCharged Insights from Top Networkers

Time to take you behind-the-scenes. Here, you are going to read the advice and insights from some of the most successful people and the best networkers I know, directly from them and in their own voices. I have included their photo, their biography, and their contact details so you can find and connect with them easily. I would highly encourage you to reach out to them, introduce yourself and start a conversation. Make sure to mention that you found out about them through this book and I am sure they will be happy to respond and continue the conversation.

Seriously, you can't just finish reading a book on networking and then not act on it. I am literally giving you access to my network. I am not going to get any real benefit if you reach out and connect with the Super Achievers here. I am doing this to add value to you. However, I am also trusting you to not mistreat the people that I care about. If you have read this far, then I hope that you will treat them with respect and that you will come from a place of Care, Value, and Service.

A great idea would be to first act on their advice, follow the 'Golden Rules', and then reach out to them. Start by introducing yourself and that you read about them in this book. Thank them for their advice and tell them how you acted on it and what results it yielded. Follow them on social media, check out their websites, platforms, and media appearances so you can bring value to the conversation from the start. Bring a million-ton of curiosity and be interested in who they are and what they are working on right now. In an ideal world, you will act on the lessons from this book and figure out a way to add value to them.

This is your chance to upgrade the 5 people you spend the most time with, expand your Sphere of Influence, expose yourself to different 'clusters' and start creating exciting new opportunities for yourself to build a vibrant and exciting future by TurboCharging your life.

"We are the opening verse of the opening page of the chapter of endless possibilities." Rudyard Kipling

Dorie Clark

Recognised as a Top 50 Business Thinkers in the world and #1 Communication Coach in the world, Dorie Clark is an adjunct professor at Duke University's Fuqua School of Business and the author of Entrepreneurial You, Reinventing You and Stand Out. New York Times described her as an "expert at self-reinvention." A former presidential campaign spokeswoman and frequent contributor to the Harvard Business Review, she consults and speaks for Google, Microsoft, and the World Bank.

Website:www.dorieclark.com
TEDx talk – https://bit.ly/3tpDC6g
Social Media Handles (Twitter, Instagram): @dorieclark
LinkedIn: @doriec
Facebook: @dorieclarkauthor

Networking Insight

"One of my most successful networking strategies is interviewing people. Especially early in your career, you may hesitate to share your own ideas - or even know what they are! But you can always interview and profile people you admire. That helps you learn from them, as well as build a personal connection. It's even better if you can leverage the power of a brand they've already heard of, such as writing for a business or industry publication. But even if that's not possible, you can start your own podcast or live-stream and a surprising number of influential people will be happy to accept your invitation, especially if they have a new offering (such as a book or movie or podcast) they want to promote."

Dr. Arayeh Norouzi

Dr. Arayeh has a Ph.D. in psychology with a focus on mindfulness. She is a rapid transformational coach, mindful living conscious parenting speaker, and corporate mindfulness trainer. She is  endorsed by Dr. Shefali Tsabary, the founder of conscious parenting and Oprah Winfrey's favorite parenting expert.

Website: www.drarayeh.com
Social Media Handles (LinkedIn, Facebook, Instagram, Twitter): @drarayeh

Networking Insight

"Ram Dass, the author of the seminal book, Be Here Now, said, *"We're all just walking each other home."* And this could very well be the best tip when it comes to networking. Transcending the façade of separation and choosing cooperation over competition is the most conscious strategy to live and do business. When we come from a place of compassion and service, connecting with like-minded people not only fulfills our basic psychological need of relatedness but enhances the quality of our vision and mission. It is easy to lose sight of our original aspiration and inner drive and chase our tails when it comes to building up our business and expanding our network. Therefore, it is critical to perpetually choose collaboration over rivalry, abundance over lack mentality, compassion over judgment, service over personal gain, humility over arrogance, and faith over fear. As Tony Robbins said, *"Business is a spiritual game."* Let us not lose sight of this gem of advice!"

G. Brian Benson

G. Brian Benson is an award-winning and #1 best-selling self-improvement and children's book author, actor, filmmaker, project coach, and TEDx speaker. As a 4x Ironman triathlete and cross-country bicyclist, Brian knows the value of hard work and never giving up on his dreams, a message he shares with audiences through each of his creative expressions. Brian's brand-new book *"Habits for Success – Inspired Ideas to Help You Soar"* is an Amazon #1 Best-Seller and was selected as a 2019 Book Excellence Award Winner in the Motivational book category.

Website: www.gbrianbenson.com
Social Media Handles (LinkedIn, YouTube, Instagram, Twitter): @gbrianbenson
Facebook: @gbrianbensonmedia

Networking Insight

- Be a good listener.
- Be You! Be authentic...you will stand out.
- Think outside the box. Get creative.
- Be equitable and give value.
- Be reliable and a person of your word.
- Make it interesting and fun.
- Get comfortable being in front of others. Join Toastmasters or take some community college speech classes. You will gain confidence!

Gene McNaughton

(At the time of writing this book Gene was extremely busy and was unable to provide a networking Tip. Therefore, with Gene's blessing, I am including Gene's top tip from his interview on my YouTube show)

Gene is an International Bestselling Author of 'The Sales E.D.G.E' and is recognised as one of the most effective Business Growth Experts. Gene helped Gateway Computers go from a small obsolete company to an $11 billion International powerhouse that was widely known for having one of the most successful sales forces in history. Gene's success at Gateway led him to become the dynamic leader of Tony Robbins' global sales force – where under his leadership, every team broke sales records that spanned over 29 years. Gene also had the privilege of being one of the opening speakers to Tony Robbins' cornerstone event, "Unleash the Power Within." Gene has worked with Giants of the Personal Development world, like Tony Robbins, John Assaraf, and Chet Holmes.

https://www.thesalesedge.co
www.growthsmart.com
Twitter, Instagram: @genemcnaughton

Networking Insight

"You never know where an introduction can take you. Most people don't do anything when they meet people. They don't follow up, or send a 'Thank You' note, or send them an email, or ask them to go and have another cup of coffee. When you meet somebody, follow up. Don't talk about yourself, talk about them."

Neal S. Phalora

Neal is a serial entrepreneur, speaker, relationship mentor, and Life Healer. Neal's coaching work has been featured in several national TV spots, Unfair Advantage Live (NYC PR networking group), Huffington Post, Walk the Talk Speaker (Ted like talk), and a multitude of podcasts. He takes his 10-year background in life coaching and brain science to help his clients with TheBrainWarrior Method (TM).

LinkedIn: @neal-phalora-thebrainwarrior
Facebook: @phalora + @NealPhalora
Instagram: @thebrainwarrior
Website: www.thebrainwarrior.com
Email: neal@thebrainwarrior.com

Networking Insight

"Be disruptive in the way in which you connect with people. Social connection it's very habituated in our brains. We get stuck in ruts in how we both approach and answer the calls of networking. I let people know that human real estate is my most valuable asset. It opens the networking with a connection and a vulnerability. I ask them that I would love to know more about their magic in the zone of genius. I will include details from their social media status or post that made a difference for me. We love to be with others because meeting people put us in awe of what is possible in each of us. Lean more into the magic when you're networking."

Sue De Caro

Sue is a heart-centered coach, educator, motivational speaker, and International Bestselling Author, working with individuals, corporations, and families around the globe to navigate life's daily challenges.

Sue has had writings featured in various online publications and magazines. She has presented at events featuring Dr. Shefali Tsabary, Neale Donald Walsch, Marianne Williamson, Anita Moorjani, and John O'Sullivan. Sue has been an invited guest on radio shows and podcasts and has also appeared on Television, on The Dr. Nandi Show, as well as, a number of appearances on FOX 29, Good Day Philadelphia.

Websites:www.suedecaro.com
www.decaroparentcoaching.com
Email: sue@suedecaro.com
Private Facebook Group - Conscious Parents, Thriving Kids

Networking Insight

"Networking does not have to connotate something negative or difficult. Look at it as an opportunity to meet someone new, learn about their work and business and if it seems in alignment with yours, perhaps you can discuss collaborating. Don't start with an agenda."

Samba Schutte

Samba Schutte is a Dutch/Mauritanian comedian, actor, and writer who was raised in Ethiopia. He starred alongside Kal Penn on the NBC sitcom "Sunnyside", executive produced by Michael Schur (The Good Place, The Office, Brooklyn Nine-Nine). He won the biggest national comedy award in Holland, and was a correspondent and writer on the Dutch version of 'The Daily Show'. He has also appeared in multiple AAA video games.

Website: www.sambaschutte.com
Social Media Handles (Instagram, Twitter & Facebook): @sambaschutte

Networking Insight

"Whenever you're trying to network with a high profile person and have a chance to talk to them, connect with them on a personal level. And sincerely. Everyone has hobbies, passions, family, favorite things you can connect with. For example, I look up producers I'm about to audition for and if they've worked on a project that had a personal impact on me, I let them know that during the audition. Like, "Hey I see you worked on 'x', and I used to watch that show back when I lived in Ethiopia. We had one TV channel back then and I remember sitting there thinking, 'Man, I can't wait to try that dish once I move to America!'" If you're sincere and make it personal, and show genuine interest in the person, you leave a good and positive impression that will make them remember you fondly. And adding some humor always helps!"

Don Wettrick

Don Wettrick is an Innovation Coordinator at Noblesville High School and is the President and founder of the StartEdUp Foundation- a non-profit empowering teen entrepreneurs. He is the author of "Pure Genius: Building a Culture of Innovation". Don has worked as a middle school and high school teacher;  educational and innovation consultant; and educational speaker. He also hosts the StartEdUp podcast, where he interviews top entrepreneurs and thought leaders like Seth Godin, Gary Vaynerchuk, Steven Kotler, and Daniel Pink. Don has lectured across the US and Europe about collaboration, social media use, and work environments that enable innovation. Most importantly Don works with educators and students to bring innovation and collaborative skills into education.

Website: startedupinnovation.com
Podcast: http://www.startedupinnovation.com/podcast

Networking Insight

"Networking is easier if you have a mission that matters. Wanting to connect for the sake of connecting is to many people- pointless. If you are working toward something that inspires, taking on a challenge that makes a difference, then networking becomes not only easier, but authentic."

Kai Whiting

Kai Whiting is the author of "Being Better: Stoicism for a World Worth Living in". He is a researcher and lecturer in sustainability and Stoicism based at UCLouvain, Belgium.

Kai is featured in numerous articles on Stoicism, including articles on DailyStoic.com and Medium.com. Kai was also featured on The Stoic Psychology Podcast, with a 3-part interview over 3 episodes and Gregory B. Sadler's YouTube show. Kai also spoke at StoiCon 2018 on Stoicism and Sustainability. Kai is a SuperConnector and takes a very practical approach to networking and build relationships with people.

Twitter: @kaiwhiting
Blog: www.StoicKai.com
Book: https://amzn.to/3cWAGYV

Networking Insight

"Engage with kindness and an open mind. Networking isn't only about opening doors, but also enjoying the room you are in."

Clement McGrath

"I have been practicing as a Healer and Transformational Life Coach for the past 38 years. After leaving a secure government job in 1984, I embarked upon what has been the most incredible journey and adventure. In 2001 I co-founded Life Coach Associates which for 14 years offered a comprehensive transformational life coach training course, training dozens of incredibly talented coaches, who in turn are helping others to transform their lives."

Email: clement@miraclesandmastery.net
Website: www.miraclesandmastery.net
Facebook: @clement.mcgrath.96

Networking Insights

1. "Make networking a top priority in your business. It needs to be one of those things that you cannot afford to let slip or neglect. A fundamental action step for any business is to generate and follow up on leads.

Networking is probably the most effective way to generate leads. Whatever your area of interest or business, do your research and identify key people in that area, and network with them.

One key concept in being successful is to work on your leverage points. These are the action steps and areas of focus that will move the needle the most. No matter what your industry, networking is an essential leverage point.

161

2. Networking is about cultivating relationships. The last thing you want to do when you connect with someone is to try and sell them something or try to convince them how brilliant you are at what you do.

The two absolutely important attitudes are:

➤ See it as building a relationship that will deepen and grow over time. It is not a quick fix approach when it comes to networking

➤ Make it about them. See where you can help them and add value to what they are doing.

When you have these attitudes, the vast majority will reciprocate. If they do not, and just want to take all they can get, then it is probably not a relationship you want to pursue. But my experience has been that those "takers" are few and far between.

The vast majority will meet you halfway and will want to grow a meaningful mutually beneficial relationship"

Catherine B Roy

Catherine B. Roy is the Founder of LHM International, a Business and Personal Growth Coach with a client base in 14 countries, and a Bestselling Author. Catherine is officially certified by the Goldman Sachs' 10,000 Women Program for business development and has received the Top 20 Global Thought Leaders and Influencers in Future at Work, Top 150 Women B2B Thought Leaders You Should Follow in 2021, Top 100 Global Thought Leaders, and Influencers in B2B and Top 30 Under 30 Young Leaders awards.

Catherine's writings are published in The Huffington Post, Thrive Global, Simple Reminders, McGill Media, Shining Mentor Magazine, Guided Mind, and many others.
As a bLU Talks speaker, she had the honour to share a virtual stage with Lisa Nichols and Les Brown.

Social Media Handles (LinkedIn, Insta, Twitter, and Clubhouse) @catherinebroy
Freebie-Top LinkedIn Strategies eBook: www.catherinebroy.com

Networking Insight

"People love to work with people. People don't decide with whom they want to work only strategically, but based on emotions too, so they choose to work with us if they trust us and if they believe we bring value to the table. I don't approach networking strategically because I can sense when someone does that and I am absolutely not going to work with such a person. I approach 1:1 with honesty, kindness, and integrity. For me, the best space to network is LinkedIn."

Corey Poirier

Corey Poirier is a multiple-time TEDx, MoMondays and PMx, Speaker. He is also the host of the top-rated 'Let's Do Influencing' Radio Show, founder of The Speaking Program, founder of bLU Talks, and he has been featured in multiple television specials and he is a Barnes and Noble, Amazon, Apple Books, and Kobo Bestselling Author.

A columnist with Entrepreneur and Forbes magazine, he has featured in/on CBS, CTV, NBC, ABC, is a Forbes Coaches Council member, and is one of the few leaders featured twice on the popular Entrepreneur on Fire show.

He has also interviewed over 6,500 of the world's top leaders and he has spoken on-site at Harvard.

Websites: www.thespeakingprogram.com   and www.blutalks.com
Email: conversationswithleaders@gmail.com

Networking Insight

"When you're networking, make sure to note important personal details about the person you spoke with so in future meetings or calls, you can reference those personal details. They will be blown away at your attention to detail and that you truly listened (and somehow remembered) what they shared with you. You can simply do this by making a few quick notes after your conversation."

Yvonne Dyson

Yvonne is a Holistic Therapist from New Zealand who thrives on challenges to create shifts. Her previous work has included at-risk youth, work within men's prison, and facilitating coaching training programmes.

Yvonne now focuses on working with women in a range of mediums with 1:1 coaching, workshops, and retreat settings. Outside of her coaching, Yvonne sings in a rock band and duo, combining confidence, creativity, and a love of music.

Website: http://thebeyond.co.nz/

Networking Insight

"Be genuine. Make genuine connections and come from a place of service. The days of spammy cold selling are well over! Sure, advertise your stuff - you have to, but people are more interested than ever in who the person is behind the pitch. This does not, of course, mean that you nail everything 100% of the time, you rather know your direction and strive towards it, while taking brutal ownership of the fact you are human!

Whether it's in terms of business or simply connecting, people remember how they feel when they are around you. There is huge power when you take the time to truly listen to someone... I'm not talking about YOU wielding the power; I'm talking about the power of connection. Magic happens when your purpose connects with their soul. We all get the choice. We can make a sale, or we can change a life."

Travis Bergren

Travis is the CEO of Rivet City Productions and Indomitus Media. Additionally, Travis is an entrepreneur and a Tech Consultant. He consults on various levels of projects ranging from technical to online product development. He leads creative projects, and co-hosts a podcast on leadership, focusing on examining leaders in nerdy fiction. When not wrestling bears or sailing his longship, Travis spends his time leading his organizations and helping companies creatively tell their stories through photo and video.

Personal: @trydus on IG

Business: @indomitusmedia on IG, Facebook, and YouTube
Business: @rivetcityproductions on IG, Facebook, and YouTube

Networking Insight

"You're only ever one or two people away from the person you most want to network with. Don't ever be afraid to leverage who you know for who you want to know. Just be considerate, and know when to do so and when not to - don't over-leverage or you might find yourself without a network at all! But don't be afraid to take risks, either. You never know when that chance meeting with someone you met a couple of years ago at a cocktail party, or your friend's significant other, might lead you to the person who brings the most value to your life."

Michael Roderick

Michael Roderick is the CEO of Small Pond Enterprises and the host of the podcast *Access to Anyone* which shows how you can get to know anyone you want in business and in life using time-tested relationship-building principles. Michael's unique methodology comes from his own experience of going from being a Highschool English teacher to a Broadway Producer in under two years. His frameworks have been featured in Forbes, Business Insider, and popular podcasts like The Art of Charm and Unmistakable Creative.

Email: michael@smallpondenterprises.com
Website: www.smallpondenterprises.com
Access to Anyone podcast: www.accesstoanyonepodcast.com
Twitter: @MichaelRoderick
LinkedIn: https://www.linkedin.com/in/michael-roderick-1161571/

Networking Insight

"Always take the time to be intentional about who you are connecting with and who you're making introductions for. Every time you make an introduction and vouch for someone, your reputation goes along with that introduction. Too many people just collect contacts and don't take the time to get to know the people they meet. If you take the time to curate and introduce great people to one another, then you'll stand out from so many others who are just playing a numbers game."

Cindy J. Cadet

Cindy J. Cadet is a relationship coach, trauma counselor, mom, and author. She helps women attract and keep healthy long-term love. She has worked with students in various capacities for over fifteen years. She is passionate about connecting with women and uplifting children. Cindy has also collaborated with her daughter to create social-emotional resources for families via Brave Kids Press.

Website: www.bravekidpressauthor.com
Instagram: @bravekidpress
YouTube: The Brave Butterfly Kid Channel

Networking Insight

"It's important to find a balance of being a giver and taker, we can't just give or just take. Both are essential for a long-lasting healthy relationship. Be authentic and vulnerable as these 2 things help to create a solid foundation."

Kelly Falardeau

Kelly Falardeau is a burn survivor since the age of 2 on 75% of her body. She found a way to go from near-death to success; from the ugly scar-faced girl to the TEDx stage twice, Fierce Woman of the Year, a 7x International Best-Selling Author, recipient of the Queen Elizabeth Diamond Jubilee Medal & YWCA Woman of Distinction. A documentary about her life story called "Still Beautiful" launched on TV plus Goalcast launched a video that has almost 10 million views. Now she is a full-time Amazon Best-Selling Strategist, coaching people to become best-selling authors. On Christmas day, Global TV announced Kelly as one of the Most Inspirational People of 2020.

Website: www.7StepsAuthor.com

Networking Insight

"Follow every single strategy in Tallal's book. Hehehe!

Seriously... Every time you meet someone, think about how you might fit into each other's world. Ask yourself these questions: Can you help them? Can they help you? If you think you can help each other, then take the next step. Don't wait for them to contact you. Contact them first. They will think you're a Super Achiever by contacting them. Remember to also follow up. That's another thing Super Achievers do... FOLLOW UP!"

William Kelley

William Kelley uses language as an interface to reprogram the mind for success and healing. He has studied the fields of Neuro-Linguistic Programming, Cognitive Behavioral Science, High performance coaching, and deep transformational therapy. He has clocked over 10,000 hours of mentoring and professional coaching. If William were quoted, he would say, "I see more potential in you than you do and my mission in life is to help get you there."

Facebook: @williaminseattle
LinkedIn: @william-kelley-900841105
Website: https://williamkelleycoaching.com/

Networking Insight

"Be a connector. Many of us go into networking with self-serving intentions which will, ironically, limit our ability to gain and attract what we want from the process of networking. Shift your mindset towards becoming a connector for others. When you network for the purpose of being able to connect others with who and what they want, you stand out because you are adding value and you build Relationship Capital.

'What are you working on and what are you struggling with?' You want to ask these 2 questions almost every time you engage someone, every day. Here's what will happen: People will probably ask you back and either: they will help you or they probably know someone who can. But you have to start with setting your intentions to be a connector, not to self-serve."

Caroline Guntur

Caroline Guntur (formerly Nilsson) is a Swedish Certified Photo Organizer and Personal Historian, specializing in digital photo organizing and family history. She is the owner of The Swedish Organizer, LLC, a company that provides customized family history solutions to clients all over the world. Caroline also hosts webinars, workshops, and creates online courses.

A native of Ystad, Sweden, Caroline has a Bachelor's Degree in Visual Communications from Hawaii Pacific University and a Master's Degree in Media Management from Columbia College Chicago. She currently divides her time between the United States and Sweden. She runs the blogs www.OrganizingPhotos.net www.SearchingScandinavia.com

Facebook: http://facebook.com/theswedishorganizer
Facebook: https://www.facebook.com/SearchingScandinavia
Instagram: https://instagram.com/theswedishorganizer
Instagram: https://www.instagram.com/searchingscandinavia
YouTube:https://youtube.com/CarolineGuntur
LinkedIn: www.LinkedIn.com/CarolineGuntur

Networking Insight

"Make one new contact every week, even if it's just to say 'Hi' and introduce yourself more. I'm introverted so I have to work on networking more, but I've started doing this lately and it's been amazing!"

171

Robert Murray

Robert Murray is a Certified High-Performance Coach and an original Master Faculty Xchange Facilitator. He's leading the "X-JET movement to eXponentially increase the levels of Joy, Engagement, and Teamwork in today's new generation of organizations. At 15, Robert Murray grew a business with a group of friends from a start-up to $200 million with the aspirational mission of being an example of how business COULD BE if it is focused on making a positive impact in the world.

Email: robhmurray@gmail.com
LinkedIn: http://www.linkedin.com/in/roberthmurray/

Networking Insight

"One of the most critical but overlooked elements of networking is your "energy"- What's going on in your inner state. More than ever, people are very aware of any inauthenticity or ulterior motives. They can "smell" fake a mile away, and it often repels them unconsciously.

You cannot ACT interested in other people. You actually have to BE interested in them. You cannot act as though you are connecting to add value to them; you have to intend to add value in every interaction. I remind myself of two critical things before going into a networking event. The first is to be fully present with the person I'm talking to, no matter what else is going on. The second is the question, "What does this person need most right now?"

I find these two questions create an "Inner State" of natural curiosity and authenticity that practically guarantees a deep connection in networking."

Bibliography

Burchard, B. (2017) *High Performance Habits – How Extraordinary People Become That Way.* Hay House

Clark, D. *"How to Become Dramatically Effective at Networking"* – LinkedIn Post https://www.linkedin.com/pulse/welcome-dorie-clark-linkedin-newsletter-dorie-clark/

Clark, D. (2015). *Stand Out Networking.* Portfolio/Penguin

Dunn, E. *"Helping Others Makes Us Happier"*- Ted Talk https://www.youtube.com/watch?v=lUKhMUZnLuw

Edwards, V. (2018) *Captivate – The Science of Succeeding with People* - Penguin

Keller, G., Papasan, J. (2012/2013) *The One Thing.* John Murray: An Hachette Uk Company. Bard Press(USA)

Lufityanto, G., Donkin, C., & Pearson, J. (2016). "Intuition – It's more than just a feeling" – Measuring Intuition: Nonconscious Emotional Information Boosts Decision Accuracy and Confidence. *Psychological Science.* doi: 10.1177/0956797616629403 https://www.psychologicalscience.org/news/minds-business/intuition-its-more-than-a-feeling.html

Randolph, R. *What Is Your Biggest Struggle With Building Professional/Personal Relationships?* – LinkedIn survey https://www.linkedin.com/posts/randolphrachel_networking-relationships-ugcPost-6812739792955027456-3V9I/

Roderick, M. *Connectorcon, Being a Super Connector and Building a World-Class Network with Michael Roderick.* Interview on 'Hustle is 4 Life Motivation' YouTube channel - https://youtu.be/9Qbeh_Uei7E

Schaefer, M. "The Relational Power of Business Networking" https://businessesgrow.com/2017/07/31/facebook-for-business-networking/

Acknowledgments

All Glory, Honour, and Thanks belong to Allah SWT, Lord of the Heavens and the Earth. I thank you for all that you have given me and I pray for your Mercy and Forgiveness.

My wife, life is pointless if you are not here by my side. Thank you for your endless love, friendship, support, and patience. You have made me better in every way and every day I aim to make you fall in love with me all over again. I probably fail more often than I succeed, but I am never going to stop trying. I can't wait to spend many more happy years with you IsA.

My son, I am so proud to see you grow up. You use all the 'Keys to Success' that we talk about and as a result, you succeed at everything that you try. I love all the time that we spend together and the deep conversations that we have. You are very strong, yet gentle and kind. Giving up is something that you know nothing of and I can't wait to see what great heights you will achieve in this life IsA.

My daughter, you bring me endless joy every day. Your kindness, generosity, and determination are endless and your smile melts my heart every time. I am proud of you for always being willing to try anything and I am surprised by how quickly you learn and master everything. I really look forward to seeing you conquer new horizons IsA.

My mother and father in-law,. Thank you for your love and for accepting me into your family. I am extremely grateful to have you in my life.

My brother-in-law, you are like a real brother to me. Your energy is infectious and I love how deeply you think. I love our high-performance driving sessions, whilst we sing at the top of our lungs. I know that things have been hard, but I know that you will never let life put you down. You deserve happiness and your fantastical fairytale bliss, just like everyone else.

My cats, Tigger and Lexa, thank you for your companionship and love. You make each day an adventure.

My brother, Alex G, your love, support, and friendship mean more to me than words can describe. Thank you for always believing in me, even when I didn't. I have always wanted a brother and I couldn't have asked for a better one. Your generosity and kindness inspire me. I am eternally grateful to have you in my life.

My grandparents, you are not here anymore, but I hope to make you proud every day. Thank you for giving me, endless love. I miss you so much!

My auntie Tauseef, you are so special to me. You are the strongest person I know. Your strength inspires me. After everything that has happened, you still smile like the full moon and bring light into my world. Thank you for not leaving me, when everyone else did. I love you with all my heart.

My uncle Umar, your strength, positivity, and support drive us all. You must be an angel in disguise! There is no other explanation. Thank you for being the only positive male role model in my life. I aspire to be more like you every day.

My cousin, Amna, I am proud to see you grow up as a strong, successful, independent young woman. You have a kind heart and you bring happiness to everyone around you. You have been through a lot at a very young age, but your smile has never faded. I know that you will achieve great things in this life.

My family in Islamabad, Sialkot, and Abbottabad (Pakistan), distance separates us, but I have you in my heart and my mind always!

My friend and mentor, Clement McGrath, our friendship has grown over the years. Your advice and support have been invaluable. Thank you for everything that you have shared with me.

My friends, teachers, and mentors. Thank you for your contributions to helping me become the man that I am today.

My colleagues and friends. Thank you for putting up with me and my eccentric ways.

Everyone who has contributed to this book. I am very grateful to have you in my life. Thank you for your support and for believing in me.

My nephews and my niece. I am proud to see you 3 grow up and I aim to be the best role model that I can be. I know that life has not been easy for you in the past, but I know that you will work hard to make a brighter future.

My sister, we didn't have much when we were younger, but back then we did have each other.

I am extremely honoured to feature all the amazing people and their wonderful stories in this book. I am forever grateful to have met you all. Thank you for allowing me to be a part of your journey. Thank you also to everyone who agreed for me to share their stories, emails, and messages. This book would not have been possible without all of you.

Kelly Falardeau, thank you for working with me on this book. I couldn't have done it without you. When we first spoke, I was clueless about everything and you opened my eyes to what was truly possible. Your support and advice have been invaluable throughout this journey. You have a beautiful soul. I look forward to us working together again in the future.

I cannot end this section without mentioning Corey Poirier, Michael Roderick, Gene McNaughton, Dorie Clark, and others who coached, advised, and guided me along the way. I really appreciate you all!

Speaking and Coaching

To have Tallal speak at your meeting, conference, or online event, or to work with Tallal as your coach, please send your email to: TurboChargedNetworking@gmail.com

About the Author

Tallal is the host of '*Hustle is 4 Life Motivation*' YouTube show (but he is taking a break at the moment to write an awesome book), where he interviewed world-class guests to expose their expertise and their secrets. In order to bring on world-class guests on his show, Tallal dedicated himself to trying and testing high-level networking strategies. Tallal has been featured on multiple podcasts, radio shows, and "The Book of Public Speaking" by Corey Poirier (International Bestselling author).

Tallal graduated from the University of Leicester with a degree in Financial Economics. He has worked in the Education sector for many years as a Maths Lecturer. Tallal teaches Boxing on the weekend to kids, teenagers, and adults, including his own son and nephews.

Tallal's super passions are building relationship equity, creating holistic success, and cultivating a savage mindset. Tallal enjoys reading non-fiction and watching UFC. He also loves going to the gym, driving fast cars, and has an unhealthy relationship with protein shakes. Tallal lives in England, UK, with his wife, 2 kids, and 2 cats.

You can reach Tallal directly at:

Email: turbochargednetworking@gmail.com

LinkedIn: @tallal.gondal

P.S. Don't forget to leave a review on Amazon and share this book with anyone who will benefit from this message.

Printed in Great Britain
by Amazon